The "Copper Scroll" Bible

The Celestial Tree of Knowledge

Michael Hearns

ISBN 978-0-9957225-4-5

Self-Published in Dublin, Ireland.

Revised 21st December 2025

The moral right of the author has been asserted

A copy of the CIP entry for this book is available from

Trinity College Dublin, Ireland, and

The Copyright Library of Congress, Washington DC, USA

www.sevenbiblewonders.com

Table of Contents

Tables

Illustrations

Introduction

The key to decode the most puzzling mystery in biblical archaeology was as dramatic as the apple that fell on Newton's head - there was a plus **+** sign between ten of the numbers on the Dead Sea Copper Scroll. It indicated that the numbers were to be added together and that just involved simple sums. Instead of treasures in biblical talents and depths in cubits that the valuables were buried, the numbers themselves turned out to be the neutral dynamic figures. This became obvious when the ten numbers with the plus + signs were added up because the total came to 225, which compared to the orbit of Venus. The Geni was out of the bottle when the additions of the numbers that were in pre-arranged groups on the scroll had totals which compared to the orbits of the planets Mercury, Venus, Mars, Jupiter, Saturn and the solar and lunar years. Encrypted behind the facade of listed treasures on the copper scroll lay an intricate archive of astronomy.

Eventually, the numbers that were paraded as weights of gold and silver treasures in talents and the depths they were buried in cubits on the copper scroll were entered onto a spreadsheet. A picture paints a thousand words and that was what materialised when individual tables for each planet and their long-term cycles were drawn in their fixed positions on the spreadsheet. That picture was in the shape of a tree with a trunk laden with numbers as talents and cubits in the centre and the tables with the orbits of the planets and their long-term cycles as the branches.

It was possible to make those discoveries from the copper scroll because the scribes had the foresight to future proof the numbers in mathematical checksums. The use of checksums was outlined in the biblical Talmud and it involved the numbers in groups adding up to a given or recognisable total. To find the recognisable totals was aided with a prompt on the copper scroll, which led to the incredible ages of the first patriarchs in Genesis Chapter 5. Those bizarre ages proved to be the recognisable checksum totals. The attention then focused on how the scribes could have formed the numbers into groups. There were seven sets of Greek letters dispersed among the numbers on the first four columns of the scroll and they turned out to be brackets to form the groups of numbers. From there, it was an exercise in using the checksums to verify the values of missing and suspect numbers whose values were difficult to determine due to erosion on parts of the copper.

While applying the checksums, the orbits of the planets were detected together with a very unusual calendar timetable, which mapped out the future. It was time to take cognises of what had developed and structure the findings with the momentous numerical data on the copper scroll. In the analysis, 22 checksum modules were formed from the numbers and they were on the first tier with Layer A of the copper scroll. It was followed where there were 21 calendar time periods identified and they were on Layer B of the scroll. Then came the orbits and long-term cycles of the planets and their tables formed the third tier with Layer C on the scroll. The three tiers were signalled because there was a reference to a third layer on the copper scroll to justify this structure.

When those three tiers of numerical data were overlaid on each other, the magnitude of what had materialised began to dawn. Despite its simple encryption with just additions of the numbers, its final mathematical jigsaw seemed beyond the limits of mere mortals to create. Prophets like Isaiah were perceived to be divinely inspired and to elaborate on this outlook, there were four vivid configurations on the copper scroll, which were mirror images of the ancient Paleo Hebrew letters, which spelled out the autograph of YHWH.

There were several references to a secret scroll or book in the Bible and the associated text indicated that nobody including the learned, could read what was written on the document because it was sealed.[1] The copper scroll was sealed by encryption and thus, the learned of today could not read it. The prophet Isaiah seemed to have had the copper scroll in mind when he wrote as follows: *Now go, write it before them in a table, and note it on a scroll, that it may be for the time to come for ever and ever:* (Isaiah 30:8) It was quite apt because the numbers on the copper scroll had to be written on a table and the figures in the calendar timetable were about a time to come for ever and ever. In the same chapter, Isaiah also stated that we should not be defiled with treasures as follows: *Ye shall defile also the covering of thy graven images of silver, and the ornament of thy molten images of gold: thou shalt cast them away as a menstruous cloth; thou shalt say unto it, Get thee hence.* (Isaiah 30:22) Just as Isaiah had outlined, the defiling treasures of gold and silver were cast aside when the numbers were seen to be significant. The menstruous cloth introduced the menstruous cycle and ancient cultures associated that cycle with the lunar month. Just a few versus down, Isaiah stated *that the light of the moon shall be the light of the sun and the light of the sun shall be sevenfold* thus endorsing the lunar and solar time, which lay within the numerical facade.

There were many strands to this investigation and one of them was to try and identity the duplicate inventory, which was referred to at the last site on the copper scroll. The analysis had already shown that the ages of Adams generations were the recognisable totals for the checksums on the scroll and that was a foot in the door of the Old Testament. The first two numbers on the copper scroll were 40 and 17 and they identified with the story of the flood where it started on the 17th day of the second month and it rained for forty days and nights. Then it was found that, just like the numbers on the copper scroll, the dates and time periods in the flood saga were also listed very precisely. The subsequent analysis showed that those time periods in the flood saga readily configured into the same time periods as in the copper scroll calendar timetable.

The revelations continued with seven sets of burnt offerings in the Old Testament, which consisted of the numbers of bullocks, rams and lambs that were slaughtered in ceremonial rituals. Here again, the copper scroll calendar showed its almighty powers, because it helped in breaking the most brilliant form of numerical encryption ever devised. Under closer scrutiny, those numbers that were listed as the totals of animals in burnt offerings were found to form into a presentation that were the same as the principal time periods in the copper scroll calendar. It transpired that the copper scroll tables of astronomy including the calendar timetable were like a biblical Rosetta stone, because they led to deciphering the true purpose for many of the strange numbers in the Bible.

The most intriguing revelation of all was where the principal periods from the copper scroll timetable mapped out a sacred timeline from Abraham down to Jesus. A majestic aura adorned this timeline where it proved to be 777 days by 777 times long. It was mirrored by a second timeline where the days of a solar calendar were paraded as men in two enormous censuses. In effect, it was a twin-track timeline and it covered the whole sweep of biblical history. It therefore would have involved the most extensive planning operation ever conducted. By overlaying that twin-track timeline on Matthews and Lukes genealogy, it proved possibly to date particular event in biblical history, beginning with the birth of Isaac in the year 1,620 BCE and ending with Jesus in 33 CE. Not only was Jesus in the right place Bethlehem as foretold by the prophets, but he was also there at the right time in 33 CE to be the predicted Messiah.

There was therefore sufficient evidence in those revelations to suggest that the Old Testament was the duplicate inventory, which was referred to on the copper scroll. It now can be seen that the data on astronomy was so sacred, that the scribes wrote it on expensive copper knowing that it would endure longer than papyrus or animal hides. They obviously disguised the numbers as weights of gold and silver treasures in the expectation that whoever found the copper scroll would safeguard it with zeal, hoping to find the valuables. In doing so, the scribes of the copper scroll had posed the

---

[1] Book of Revelation 5:1-9, 10:2-10, Book of Isaiah 29:11, Book of Daniel 12:4 and Book of Ezekiel 2:9-10.

ultimate examination test for future biblical scholars because they would have to be educated on the higher language of the biblical writers in order to decipher the enigmatic document. Unfortunately, most scholars believed the treasures were real and many archaeological expeditions were conducted over the decades looking to find the gold and silver caches. They were in essence looking for crocs of abstract gold at the end of the rainbow especially as the descriptions of where the questionable amounts of treasures were supposed to be buried were either too vague or nonsensical.

There is an intriguing treasure trail ahead but it is to identify metaphorical gems of numbers as calendar periods or planetary orbits on the copper scroll. This may seem to be a daunting challenge especially when you browse through the book and see so many tables of figures and charts. However, this is knowledge from another world and that was the only way the author of the copper scroll could convey it. But it is only simple arithmetic that you learned at school with mainly additions and multiplications, so cherish the opportunity to learn this higher language from the copper scroll, because it was sealed by encryption and not even the learned ones could read it.

Chapter 1

The Numbers on the Copper Scroll

There were many tell-tale indications that the numbers of treasures and cubits were suspect especially as their weights and measurements were listed so precisely. Afterall, would it have mattered to rogue looters with excited imaginations, how many talents were hidden at a site when the mere whisper of treasures would have been sufficient to cause a gold rush. The oddities continued where the cubits and treasures at a site were the recognisable numbers of 7 and 22 that formed pi. To indicate that pi was intended, it was followed at the very next site were the numbers of 3, 60 and 2 multiplied out to 360, which were the number of degrees in a circle. On this route less travelled, it was noticeable at one of the sites that the numbers of cubits and treasures were the same as the numbers to form the biblical 364 days calendar year as outlined in the Book of Enoch.

Those three examples with pi, the degrees in a circle and the 364 day calendar focused the attention directly on the numbers themselves without the cubits and treasures. But that line of investigation was fraught with risk because the copper had been oxidised and eroded and therefore, its numbers could not be taken for granted as being reliable. To find out how dependable the numbers were, eight different translations of the copper scroll were referenced and remarkably, the scholars had all come up with practically the same numbers. The latest translation that was referenced was by Emile Puech and he had the advantage of conducting his research after the copper scroll had undergone comprehensive refurbishment using sophisticated technology and modern scientific techniques. In his translation, Puech had listed two extra sets of numbers, which had not been legible to the previous translators. It was between those extra numbers where the plus ✚ signs were listed.

That plus sign ✚ indicated that the numbers were to be added together and that was another indication that arithmetic was involved with the numbers on the copper scroll. Adding the numbers together was the same principle as what applies with mathematical checksums. The use of checksums was a method to future proof groups of numbers. It required that all of the numbers in a group to be added up to form a total. That total was a quick ready reckoner to recheck later if the total was still the same. If not, then the values of one or more of the individual numbers had altered when they were copied onto a new document or accidentally erased. The Jewish scribes used the principle of checksums when copying sacred documents and the rules for transcribing were laid down in the Talmud.[2]

It was outlined above how pi and a circle were the first signs of intelligent data to be detected on the copper scroll. There was more information beneath the surface with pi and a circle and it was quite revealing. The two numbers with 7 cubits and 22 talents together triggered the notion of pi which is the ratio between the diameter and the circumference of a circle. At the very next site the numbers to form the degrees in a circle were obvious where the instructions were as follows: *"Above the mouth of the water spring of Buz, in it three cubits towards the wall are buried 60 k(arsh of) s(ilver and) two talents of gold."*[3] The site has never been located because the details were just too vague. However, the numbers were clear-cut with **3** cubits, **60** karsh or talents of silver and **2** talents of gold because they multiplied out to 360 and that was the number of degrees in a circle.

---

[2] Trac Macon Sumner, p 53.
[3] Judah Lefkovits, p 234.

On reading the commentary by the translator Lefkovits it was noticed that he had referred to the *'mouth of the water'* as *'mouth opening'* relative to the quote above. Just like a circle, an open mouth can be round in shape. In the investigation a biblical search engine was employed to compare the numbers and words on the copper scroll with those on the Old Testament because it was the oldest historical source to reference. When the words *'round mouth'* was entered onto the search engine, it stopped with the only listing of those two words in the Old Testament. The location was where Solomon was building the temple and astonishingly, it was where the biblical formula to calculate pi was listed. (I Kings Chapter 7) The aim with the search words *'round mouth'* had been as accurate as the arrow of William Tell in hitting the target. The match was all the more remarkable where it was the only place in the Old Testament, which identified the ratio with pi.

The attention then focused on the numbers between the Greek letters to see if any pattern was evident or if a mathematical equation was embodied in the figures. It became noticeable that four of the numbers in the first two columns of the copper scroll had been arranged into couplets by those sets of Greek letters. However, one number stood out for it was on its own between the Greek letters HN and OE at it was 65. The number 65 was given as the first age of God's favourite patriarch Enoch who supposedly became a father at 65 years of age. (Genesis Chapter 5)

The encounter with the number 65 at the early stage of the investigation did not arouse attention until on <u>column nine</u> of the scroll there were three numbers, which were similar to numbers in the Book of Enoch. The instruction on the copper scroll was *"to measure out 13 cubits at a particular location and to find 7 talents of silver and 4 coins."* In comparison, the Book of Enoch outlined about the solar year and it listed **13** weeks of **91** days and the later period was apportioned to each of **4** leaders to multiply out to **364** days. (Enoch 74-82) The numbers on the scroll when presented without the cubits and treasures also multiplied out to 364.

Those two gems of wisdom with pi and Enoch's 364-day solar calendar undermined the concept of the copper scroll being a real treasure list and therefore, the numbers themselves became the centre of attention. It led to entering all of the numbers of cubits and the weights of the gold and silver treasures in talents onto a spread sheet as shown in Table 1. There were also miscellaneous cardinal and optimal numbers on the scroll and these were part of the instructions on where to find the hidden treasure. Examples related to such things as on the 2nd floor, on the third platform or at the four corners of a site. There were seven sets of Greek letters dispersed among the numbers in the first four columns of the scroll and they were included on the right hand side column of the tables. There were also several Greek loan words in the text on the scroll and references to three of them were included in the table. There were extra treasures at seven of the sites and they protruded like spurs and they proved to be very important and are represented with the symbol) (. Due to erosion on parts of the copper, there were eight of the numerical values of the treasures, which translators found difficult to determine and they are highlighted in pink colour.

How thrilling it is to view the layout of the important data on the copper scroll. The evidence will indicate that there was an original copy of this data and it most likely was on papyrus or animal hides. Excluded were the descriptions of the hiding places where the treasures were supposed to be hidden for they were a clever ruse. But some of the details seemed to amplify the particular findings by pointing to locations in the Old Testament.

In this investigation, eight English translations of the copper scroll were referenced and they were by John Allegro, Garcia Martinez, Al Wolters, Michael Wise, Giza Vermes, JT Milik, Judah Lefkovits and Emile Puech. While the individual descriptions by the translators of the various sites were often different, it was noticeable that they had successfully identified the same values for practically all of the numbers. The most recent translation of the copper scroll was by Emile Puech in 2006 and revised in 2015. The translation took place after an extensive restoration process on the copper scroll. All the advantages of modern sophisticated technology were applied in trying to enhance and reproduce the original text.

The tables of figures may look daunting but they are mainly for reference only. As you proceed to the checksums and to the calendar timetable, the numbers involved are presented in tables and are listed starting in a particular row and ending in a particular row. Therefore, the rows are the way into the tables and the rest is just the addition of the numbers. Those additions are already done in the forthcoming tables so it is their totals that matters.

Puech was able to identify two extra groups of numbers the first of which were 20 + 20 + (?) + 14 in <u>column four</u>. There was one number on that list, which Puech was unable to identify because of erosion. The second group of numbers in the translation by Puech were 20 +20 + (20?) + 22 and they were in <u>column six</u> of the scroll. One of the numbers seemed to be suspect because he had placed a question mark after it (20?).

Table 1: The Numbers on the Copper Scroll.

Column	Miscellaneous	Cubits	Row	Treasures Site	Treasure Numbers	Greek Letters	Spurs
1	A chest	40	1	Talents	17	KEN	
	3rd Layer		2	Gold Ingots	100	Peristyle	
			3	Talents	900		
	Sabbatical year	6	4			ΧΑΓ	
		3	5	Silver Talents	40		
2			6	Talents	42	HN	
	3rd Layer		7	Gold Ingots	65	OE	
			8	Silver Talents	70		
	Spur of rock	15	9	Talents	10	ΑΙ	
			10	Silver Bars	6		
	East	4	11	Talents	22		
3	South	9	12	S & G Pieces	609	Peribolos	
	North	16	13	Silver Karsh	40	TP	
	Western		14				
	14 was correct number	3	15	Silver Karsh	14 ?		
4	Missing number was 32		16	Silver karsh	20+20+(?)+14		ΣK
	14 was correct number	14 ?	17	Silver Karsh	55		
	2 cavities	3	18	Pots of Silver	2		
			19	Silver Karsh	200		
			20	Silver Karsh	70		
		1	21	Silver Karsh	12		
5		3	22	Silver Karsh	7		
			23				
		3	24	Silver Karsh	23		)(
		7	25	Silver Karsh	32		
6	An Urn, a Book	3	26	Silver Karsh	42		
		9	27	Silver Karsh	21		
		12	28	Silver Karsh	27		
	Suspect number was 14	9	29	Silver Karsh	20+20+(14 ?)+22		)(
7	4 Sides	24	30	Talents	400		
		6	31	Silver Bars	6		
		7	32	Silver Karsh	22		
	Correct number was 60	3	33	Siver karsh	60 Or 80 ?	2	)(
8	a Silver bar was correct		34		1 bar ?		Note
	Stone Monument	17	35	Silver Karsh	17		
		3	36	Silver Karsh	7		
		24	37	Silver Karsh	66		
		11	38	Silver Karsh	70		
9	2 hole	13	39	Bars of Silver	7	4	)(
	2nd Terace	8 ½	40	Silver Karsh	23 ½		
		16	41	Silver Karsh	22		
	a mina was correct		42		I MINA ?		Note
		7	43	Silver Karsh	9		
			44				
9 / 10	2nd level		45	Silver Karsh	9		
10			46	Silver Karsh	12		
		10	47	Silver Talents	62		
		2	48	Gold Talents	300	20	)(
		12	49	Silver Karsh	80		
	4 Corners		50	Silver Karsh	17		
11			51				
	A tally		52				
			53				
			54	Silver Karsh	40		
	A tally		55				
	3 cubits was correct	3 ?	56				
			57	Silver Talents	900	Triclinum	
	a tally		58	Silver Karsh	5	60	)(
12			59	Talents	42		
	One Chest		60	Silver Karsh	60		
			61	G&S Talents	600		
			62	Talents	71	20	)(
			63	A Duplicate Copy			

The exercise with applying the checksums identified the values of missing and suspect numbers that were illegible due to erosion of the copper. There were in all ten exceptions between Puech and the other translators on the values of the numbers and remarkably, the true values were determined by the checksums. Puech had a different listing of numbers for the various sites than most of the other translators. Because the decoding exercise involves numbers on spreadsheet tables, it was necessary to stress that the original sites are listed as rows in this analysis and presented from Row 1 to Row 63.

- Puech had identified the number 14 at Row 15 instead of 13 by other translators. The checksums proved that 14 was the correct number.

- Puech had identified that there were four numbers on Row 16 one of which was unidentifiable. Those numbers were 20 + 20 + (?) + 14 and the checksums proved that 32 was the missing number and it will be applied in the analysis. The other translators had just identified one number with 14 only on that row.

- Puech had identified the number 14 at Row 17 instead of several different values by the other translators. The checksums proved that 14 was the correct number.

- On Row 29, Puech had identified that there were four numbers and these were 20 + 20 + (20?) + 22. There was one number (20?) that was suspect and the checksums proved that the true value was 14 and it will be applied in the analysis. The other translators were only able to identify one number on that row but had various values for it.

- On Row 33, Puech had listed 80 Silver Karsh whereas four other translators had 60 talents. (Vermes p 629, Martinez p 462, Lefkovits p 234, Wolters) It transpired with the checksums that 60 was the correct number.

- On Row 34, there were three translators who had *'a silver bar'* but Puech did not. (Martinez p 462, Vermes p 629, Wolters) The checksums indicated that a silver bar counting as *one silver bar* was correct and it was applied in the analysis.

- On Row 36, Puech had 7 Silver Karsh whereas some translators had 4 talents. It transpired with the checksums that 7 was the correct number.

- On Row 42, there were three translators who had 'a mina' but Puech did not. (Martinez p 462, Wise p 196, Wolters) The checksums indicated that a mina counting as *one mina* was correct and it is applied in the analysis.

- On Row 56, Lefkovits had 3 cubits whereas none of the other translators including Puech had any cubits on that row. (Lefkovits p 392) The checksums indicated that the 3 cubits were correct at it was applied in the analysis.

- Puech had *'one tithe vessel of aloes'* on Row 56 but not so with the other translators. A tithe vessel of aloes was not a gold or silver treasure but instead was possibly oil used in anointing. It therefore did not feature in the checksum formations.

In case some readers are moving out of their comfort zone with these numbers and checksums, it is necessary to make a statement in order to put them at ease. This is a decoding exercise and it will show that the numbers on the copper scroll were the real treasures for behind their façade lay a wonderful knowledge from antiquity. Instead of poring over vague archaic coordinates on a map or pining to understand the trappings from the elves of folklore, the challenge was to comprehend the logic and technicalities of the encrypted numbers.

Brackets

The initial part of the analysis showed that the Greek letters acted as brackets to contain the numbers in sequence to form the checksum totals with the ages of the patriarchs. But that only covered the first four columns of numbers on the scroll. Therefore, it required identifying more markers that would act as brackets on the remaining eight columns on the scroll.

It transpired that the scribes had used Enoch as the tour guide to provide more checksum brackets with the various indices to form his ages and with his solar calendar. It began where his first age of 65 was singled out as the only number on its own between the two sets of Greek letters HN and OE. Just before the number 65 were the numbers 40 and 42 and they were between the Greek letters ΧΑΓ and HN. Following the number 65 were the numbers 70 and 10 and they were between the Greek letters OE and ΔI. Those four numbers added up to 162, which was the age of Jared when his son Enoch was born. The scribes of the copper scroll showed their creativity where they had split the age of Jared at 162 into two modules so that they formed brackets around Enoch with his first age of 65 in the middle as shown in the image below.

ΧΑΓ   40   42   HN   65   OE   70   10   ΔI

**Total of 40 + 42 + 70 + 10 = 162. Age of Jared when
Enoch was born**

There was more to follow because Puech had identified the two sets of numbers in sequence on <u>row sixteen</u> and <u>row twenty-nine</u> on the scroll with the plus signs + and that indicated the numbers were to be added. When the two groups of numbers were added together including the values of 32 and 14 for the missing and suspect numbers, the result was 162 as shown below.

20 + 20 + (32) + 14 plus 20 + 20 + (14) + 22 = 162

The fingerprints of Enoch were again evident because the number 162 was the equivalent of the age of Jared when his son Enoch was born. Therefore, there was the age of Enoch at 65 when Methuselah was born and now the age of Jared at 162 when Enoch was born.

On Row 24 the instruction was to go 60 cubits and then a further 3 cubits and that was 60 + 3 cubits. It was the only row or site that had two listing of cubits and notably, it was between those two extra lists of numbers that had been detected by Puech. Those two lists of numbers had added to 162 above and by adding 63, the total came to 225. It was the orbits of Venus around the sun and therefore, it was the second recognisable number to be a checksum total. The other recognisable total was with the final age of Enoch at 365.

Enoch was setting a track record and a cursory study of the other numbers down the copper scroll revealed that they had been prearranged to act as brackets to form more checksums. The brackets were as follows:

1. The first appearance with Enoch was with the number 65 and it was the only number on its own that was between two sets of Greek letters, which were HN and OE. On one side

of 65 were the numbers 40 and 42 and on the other side were 70 and 10 and they were both between two sets of Greek letters. Those numbers added up to 162 and that was the age of Jared when his son Enoch was born. The split age of Jared symbolised two brackets around Enoch. It set the scene for applying other brackets with Enoch when forming the sequences with the checksum totals and calendar indices.

2. On <u>rows twelve</u> and <u>thirteen,</u> were the number 9, 16 and 40 and they added up to 65, which was the first age of Enoch. The number 16 and 40 on <u>row thirteen</u> ended with the Greek letters TP which was making a mission statement. Because the Greek letters TP were to act as a bracket, then the numbers that partially added up to Enoch's age on the same row were intended to also act as a bracket.

3. The numbers 20 + 20 + 32 + 14 were just before the Greek letters ΣK on <u>row sixteen</u> and when added to 20 + 20 + 14 + 22 on row twenty nine, the total at 162 was the first age of Jared when his son Enoch was born. Even from birth, Enoch had been utilised by the scribes to perform a role with brackets. In this case, it showed that the numbers with the plus + signs on <u>row sixteen</u> had acted as a bracket because the total of all the numbers beginning on <u>row sixteen</u> and ending on <u>row twenty nine</u> added up to 777. This was a confirmation that the extra treasures that formed spurs were to be utilised as brackets to form the numbers into groups.

4. The third spur or bracket was where the numbers 3, 60 and 2 on <u>row thirty three</u> added up to 65, which equated to the first age of Enoch.

5. The fourth spur or bracket was with the indices to form the biblical 364-day calendars on <u>row thirty nine</u> with the numbers 13, 7 and 4. Those three numbers multiplied out to 364 and this equation was shown in the Book of Enoch.

6. The equivalent number of Enoch's second age of 300 years was on <u>row forty eight</u> to act as a bracket.

7. On <u>row fifty-nine</u> there were the two numbers of 60 and 5 and they added up to 65, which was the equivalent of Enoch's first age. The two numbers also multiplied out to 300 which was the equivalent of Enoch's second age.

There hidden in plain sight with Enoch lay the configuration of numbers to form the calendar timetable on the copper scroll together with the brackets. In the Book of Enoch, it outlined that the patriarch was shown the heavenly tablets. Because of the significant role that can be attributed to Enoch relative to the formation of checksums and calendar indices, it would indicate that the copper scroll matrix of numbers were those tablets.

The Number of Cubits on the Copper Scroll

The total of the numbers of the gold and silver talents together with the numbers of items such as vessels were then added up for the various translators. Because numbers were the main focus of this investigation, I checked for signs of recognisable values but no identifiable results emerged. I also added up the number of cubits on the scroll. Instead of cubits, three of the translators had listed notches on rows 47, 48 and 49 on the scroll. However, the latest translation was by Puech and he had identified them as cubits. The results with the totals of cubits and notches are shown in Table 2.

The listing of the cubits shows that three of the translators had practically arrived at the same totals. The total for Puech was 383.5 and Wise was 382.5. Wolters had listed 22 notches instead of cubits but when both cubits and notches were added together, his total came to 380.5. It should be noted that Lefkovits had listed 3 cubits in column eleven whereas the other translators had not. The checksums had validated that the 3 cubits were correct and that they were originally on the scroll. This was added to the total cubits by Puech and made it **386.5** cubits.

Table 2: The Cubit Measurements.

	Total Cubits	Total Notches	Cubits + Notches
Peuch	383.5	0	383.5
Wise	382.5	0	382.5
Wolters	358.5	22	380.5
Vermes	390	22	412
Martinez	388	22	410
Allegro	360.5	0	360.5

The copper scroll was written at least two thousand years ago which means we have to tread cautiously when evaluating their numerical content. Imagine if the numbers were written in Roman numerals like we see on some clock faces where V = 5, X = 10 or on an old buildings with the inscription of MDCCLXXVI. That is a measure of how numbers have changed since the time of Jesus. We employ calculators whereas in ancient times they used an abacus or mathematical references tables. We count in tens, hundreds and thousands in the metric system because it is far simpler to multiply or divide. But there are other systems still in use such as with weights and measures. Therefore, when dealing with ancient numerical systems it is sometimes better to revert back to basics and imagine you had to count on your fingers or an abacus.[4]

---

[4] For an understanding of ancient mathematics reference *Neugebauer, O. The Exact Sciences in Antiquity, New York, Dover 1969 and* McLeish John *Number*, Published by Bloomsbury, London WIV 5DE 1991.

Chapter 2

The Checksums Verify the Numbers were Intact

If the scribes of the copper scroll had encased the numbers in checksums, then there were two main elements to watch out for. The numbers in checksums have to be arranged into specific groups while the totals of those numbers had to be recognisable. The possibility of forming specific groups focused the attention on seven sets of Greek letters that were dispersed among the numbers at the beginning of the copper scroll because they seemed ideal to serve that purpose. The challenge then was to see if identifiable totals could be found.

The Greek letters also aided this quest where there was only one number between HN and OE and it was 65. That number was recognisable as the first age of Enoch when he became a father to Methuselah as outlined in Genesis Chapter 5. A recognisable number was required to behave as a checksum total and the final age of Enoch's at 365 years was perfect for that role because it was also the number of days in a solar year.

The investigation had been led into the chapter in the Book of Genesis where the unbelievable ages of the first patriarchs where listed with most of them having lived to be over 900 years old. It seemed peculiar that the inscriptions of how long those men lived were like the way names and ages were displayed on tombstones. The notion of tombstones was prompted by the copper scroll because it stated that a duplicate inventory was buried in a cave with tombs at its mouth and the ages of the patriarchs were at the beginning or mouth of the Old Testament.

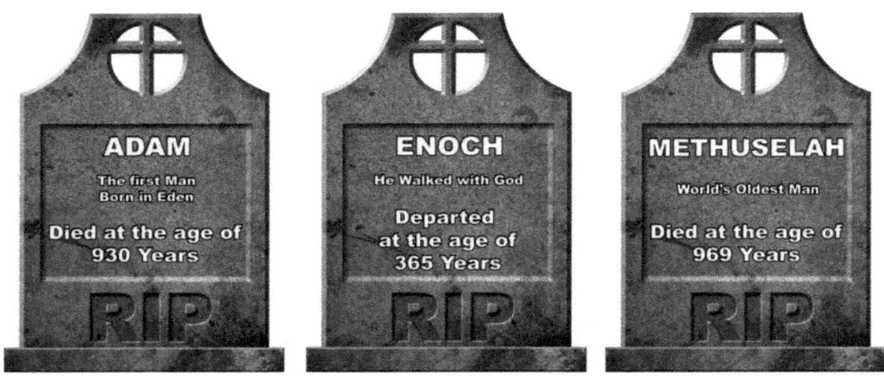

Those ages were in the realms of fantasy such as where Methuselah became a father to Lamech when he was 187 years old and he lived to be the world's oldest man at 969 years of age. Methuselah's son Lamech lived to be 777 years old. In turn, the son of Lamech was none other than Noah and he supposedly lived to be 950 years old.

'*As old as Methuselah*' was the catchphrase and his final age of 969 years was tried to see if it might be a checksum total? It was then found that all of the numbers of treasures and the cubits between the Greek letters HN and ΣK added up in sequence to a total of 937. That number was short of Methuselah's final age of 969 years by 32. However, there was one number missing because it had been too eroded for Puech to determine its value. If the final age of Methuselah was indeed a checksum total, then that missing number would be 32. To verify that 32 was the original value, a second checksum in parallel would be required.

The next attempt to identify a checksum began at the Greek letters ΔI and by adding the numbers of treasures down to the Greek letters ΣK, the total came to 745. This total was 32 short of 777, which was the final age of Methuselah's son Lamech. It was the second checksum in which 32 had featured for the missing number and so it was an indication that it was the original value. The analysis continued and it was found that the total of the treasures between the Greek letters TP and ΣK added up to 100 and this number was equal to the first age of Noah's son Shem. That total also included the missing number with its possible value of 32. It was the biblical imperative of a third witness to indicate that the missing number was indeed 32.

Those checksums had done their duty because they had confirmed the value of the missing number was 32. In due course, several checksums were formed by applying the ages of the first patriarchs and they covered the numbers between sets of the Greek letters on the first four columns of the copper scroll. Thereafter, there was an obstacle confronting the investigation because it required more brackets like the Greek letters to form groups on the last eight columns of the copper scroll. It was back to the drawing board but eventually, a solution was detected. It turned out that there were seven sites where a second set of treasures were listed and they jutted out like spurs on the spreadsheet copy of the copper scroll. Those spurs were well positioned to be extra brackets and they were confirmed as intended where the numbers of cubits and treasures added up to the ages of Enoch or multiplied to form his calendar indices of 364 days.

By applying those spurs as brackets to form groups, the checksum exercise continued and it showed a wonderful foresight by the biblical scribes where it proved possible to confirm the original values of all of the numbers on the copper scroll. So far, a total of 23 checksums were formed from the numbers on the copper scroll and they are set out in tables to make it easy for the reader to verify the results.

Those 23 checksums will now be outlined in detail and how their totals compared to the ages of Adam's generations, which are shown in Table 3. The first age was when each man became a father while the second age was how long they lived thereafter and the third age was how old they were when they died. The one exception was again with Enoch for the Bible says he did not die for God took him supposedly to his heavenly dominion.

Table 3: The Ages of Adam's Generations in Years

Names	1st Age	2nd Age	Final Age
Adam	130	800	930
Seth	105	807	912
Enos	90	815	905
Cainan	70	840	910
Mahalaleel	65	830	895
Jared	162	800	962
Enoch	65	300	365
Methuselah	187	782	969
Lamech	182	595	777
Noah	500	450	950

The <u>first</u> checksum table was with Methuselah and it consisted of the numbers of cubits and treasures in the mini-group, which was formed by the Greek letters HN and ΣK as shown in Table 4. To get the total of Methuselah's age of 969, it required inserting 32 for a missing number on Row 16. But it needed a second and third example running in parallel to verify that 32 was the value of the missing number.

The total of the treasures only with the numbers in sequence between the Greek letters ΔI and ΣK added up to 745. This total was 32 short of 777, which was the final age of Methuselah's son Lamech. The complete sequence including the number 32 for the missing number is shown in Table 5. It was the <u>second</u> checksum and it had featured the number 32 for the missing number, which was an indication that it was the original value.

Table 4: Methuselah at 969

Rows	Cubits	Treasures
		Greek Letters **HN**
7		65
8		70
9	15	10
10		6
11	4	22
12	9	609
13	16	40
14		No Numbers
15	3	14
16		20+20+(32)+14 Greek Letters **ΣK**
Totals	**47**	**922**
Grand Total = 969		

Table 5: Lamech at 777

Rows	Treasures
	Greek Letters **ΔI**
10	6
11	22
12	609
13	40
14	No Numbers
15	14
16	20+20+(32)+14 Greek Letters **ΣK**
Total = 777	

The exercise continued and it was found that the total of the treasures between the Greek letters of TP and ΣK added up to 100 and this number was equal to the first age of Noah's son Shem. The sequence of the numbers including 32 for the missing number is shown in Table 6. It was the <u>third</u> checksum and it had again featured the number 32 for the missing number.

When forming the checksum for Methuselah, I noticed that the total of the treasures from the Greek letters HN where the checksum began to the numbers 609 and 9 on <u>row twelve</u> was 782. The total of 782 was the equivalent of the second age of Methuselah and it was the <u>fourth</u> checksum total. There was a Greek loan word Peribolos where the sequence to form the total of 782 had ended and it was another type of bracket. The sequence is shown in Table 7.

Table 6: Shem at 100

Rows	Treasures
	Greek Letters **TP**
14	No Numbers
15	14
16	20+20+(32)+14 Greek Letters **ΣK**
Total = 100	

Table 7: Methuselah at 782

Rows	Treasures
	Greek Letters **HN**
7	65
8	70
9	10
10	6
11	22
12	**Greek Word Peribolos** 609
Total = 782	

The fifth checksum was the total of the treasures and cubits from the Greek letters XAΓ to the Greek loan word Peribolos, which again acted as a bracket. The sequence is shown in Table 8 and the total of 895 was equal to the final age Enoch's grandfather Mahalaleel. The next part of the exercise was to again use the Greek loan word Peribolos as a bracket and count the treasures and cubits down the copper scroll. When the count reached the Greek letters ΣK the total came to the final age of Lamech at 777 with 32 for the missing number included as shown in Table 9. This was the sixth checksum total. It was also the fourth checksum total to feature the missing numbers as 32, which was sufficient to declare it the original values of the number. It was significant where the Greek loan word Peribolos had acted as a bracket to form three checksum totals with 782, 895 and 777.

Table 8: Mahalaleel at 895

Rows	Cubits	Treasures
		Greek Letters XAΓ
5	3	40
6		42
7		65
8		70
9	15	10
10		6
11	4	22
12		Greek Word Peribolos
	9	609
Totals	31	864
Grand Total = 895		

Table 9: Lamech at 777

Rows	Cubits	Treasures
		Greek Word Peribolos
12	9	609
13	16	40
14		No Numbers
15	3	14
16		20+20+(32)+14
		Greek Letters ΣK
Totals	28	749
Grand Total = 777		

The investigation continued and it required using the seven spurs with the extra treasures as brackets on the spreadsheet copy of the copper scroll. The next checksum began with the numbers 20 + 20 + 32 + 14 on row sixteen and ended with the last number in the spur with the numbers 20 + 20 + (20?) + 22 on row twenty-nine. Puech had placed a question mark after one of the numbers with (20?) and obviously its value was suspect. If the value of the suspect number was 14 instead of 20, then the checksum total for all of the treasures and cubits from row sixteen to row twenty-nine of the scroll would add up to 777 as shown in Table 10. The total at 777 was equal to the final age of Lamech and it was the seventh checksum total. It had used the spurs with the extra numbers as the readymade brackets and both ends of the sequence.

The checksum also used the value of the missing number as 32 and this was the fifth time it had successfully completed a sequence with an age of the patriarchs. It also included the number 14 for the suspect number of (20?) as outlined by Puech. Because the suspect number had been altered to 14, there was a need to locate a second and third checksum, which would validate the number as its original value.

The eight checksum total was with the final age of Noah and the sequence immediately followed on after that last checksum with Lamech at 777. It therefore began on row thirty after a bracket with the spur and it included the treasures and cubits down to row forty seven as shown in Table 11. The total at 950 was equal to the final age of Noah. There was a bonus with this checksum with Noah and it was where the sequence had ended just before the spur, which had the number that was the same as Enoch's second age at 300 on row forty eight. Therefore, the final ages of Methuselah, his son Lamech and his grandson Noah had all been unveiled as checksum totals where they were laid out from <u>row seven</u> down to <u>row forty seven</u> on the copper scroll in the same seniority order as in the Bible.

It can be seen from those initial checksums that the numbers to form the totals were naturally all in sequence and were between brackets. There were three options to form those initial checksum sequences on the copper scroll the first of which was to use the treasures and cubits while the second was to use only the treasures. The third option was to use only the cubits. The scribes had demonstrated those three options with the three ages of Methuselah. His final age with the number 969 used both the treasures and cubits. His second age with the number 782 used only the treasures. The numbers to form Methuselah's first age was with the cubits only and they were between <u>row twenty four</u> and <u>row thirty seven</u> and the total came to 187. It was the <u>ninth</u> checksum total. The only possible sign of a bracket was where the sequence started just after <u>row twenty three</u> where there were no numbers of cubits or treasures.

Table 10: Lamech at 777

Rows	Cubits	Treasures	
16		**Plus + Sign Bracket**	
		20+20+(32)+14	ΣK
17	14	55	
18	3	2	
19		200	
20		70	
21	1	12	
22	3	7	
23		No Numbers	
24	60 + 3	23	
25	7	32	
26	3	42	
27	9	21	
28	12	27	
29	9	20+20+(14)+22	
		Plus + Sign Bracket	
Totals	**124**	**653**	
	Grand Total = 777		

Table 11: Noah at 950

Rows	Cubits	Treasures	
		Plus + Sign Bracket	
30	24	400	
31	6	6	
32	7	22	
33	3	60	2
34		**a Silver Bar**	
35	17	17	
36	3	7	
37	24	66	
38	11	70	
39	13	7	4
40	8 1/2	23 1/2	
41	16	22	
42		**a Mina**	
43	7	9	
44		No Numbers	
45		9	
46		12	
47	10	62	
		Enoch's Bracket) (	
Totals	**149.5**	**794.5**	**6**
	Grand Total = 950		

The <u>tenth</u> checksum total was with the treasures in sequence beginning after the Greek letters of OE on <u>row eight</u> and ending on <u>row seventeen</u> as shown in the top part of Table 12. The total at 912 was equal to the final age of Seth. There was no bracket at the end. It was found that the sequence continued and it formed the <u>eleventh</u> checksum total from the treasures only beginning on the very next row or <u>row eighteen</u> and continued until it ended on <u>row thirty</u> and again the total was with 912. That was two listings in complete sequence with the final age of Seth at 912 and both are shown on Table 12. It appeared that there was a particular purpose for the scribes arranging those two listings of 912 in sequence for their combined totals added up to 1,824 and this was equal to five solar years to within two days. This was an indication that the numbers on the copper scroll could also represent days.

The scribes had not finished with Seth because there was a third sequence beginning on <u>row thirty three</u> with a spur as a bracket. It continued with all the treasures and cubits to end with another spur where

Enoch's second age of 300 was listed on <u>row forty eight</u>. It was the <u>twelfth</u> checksum total at 807 and that was equal to the second age of Seth as shown in Table 13. Those three checksums with Seth had future proofed the numbers of treasures on thirty nine rows of the scroll. It was thus three super checksums with Seth.

Table 12: Seth at 912

Rows	Treasures
8	OE 70
9	10
10	6
11	22
12	609
13	40
14	No Numbers
15	14
16	20+20+(32)+14
17	55
	Total = 912
18	2
19	200
20	70
21	12
22	7
23	No Numbers
24	23
25	32
26	42
27	21
28	27
29	20+20+(14)+22
30	400
Total = 912 + 912	

Table 13: Seth at 807

Rows	Cubits	Treasures	
33	3	60	2
34		a Silver Bar	
35	17	17	
36	3	7	
37	24	66	
38	11	70	
39	13	7	4
40	8 1/2	23 1/2	
41	16	22	
42		a Mina	
43	7	9	
44		No Numbers	
45		9	
46		12	
47	10	62	
48	2	300	20) (
Grand Total = 807			

The <u>thirteenth</u> checksum total began on <u>row nine</u> and it consisted of the treasures and cubits to end on <u>row eighteen</u> with the treasures only and not the cubits in that row as shown in Table 14. The total at 905 equated to the final age of Enos at 905 years. However, there were no brackets identified to encase the sequence.

The <u>fourteenth</u> checksum total was with the final age of Cainan and it was with the treasures only from <u>row nineteen</u> down to <u>row thirty</u> giving a total of 910. The sequence is shown in Table 15 and there were no brackets identified.

Table 14: Enos at 905

Rows	Cubits	Treasures
9	15	10
10		6
11	4	22
12	9	609
13	16	40
14	No Numbers	
15	3	14
16		20+20+(32)+14
17	14	55
18		2
Totals =	61	844
Grand Total = 905		

Table 15: Cainan at 910

Rows	Treasures
19	200
20	70
21	12
22	7
23	No Numbers
24	23
25	32
26	42
27	21
28	27
29	20+20+(14)+22
30	400
Total =	910

The <u>fifteenth</u> checksum total was with the second age of Adam and Jared at 800 years and it consisted of the treasures only from <u>row twenty</u> to <u>row thirty three</u> as shown in Table 16. There was no bracket identifiable at the beginning of the sequence but it did end with a spur with the indices of Enoch's calendar.

Table 16: Adam and Jared at 800

Rows	Treasures	
20	70	
21	12	
22	7	
23	No Numbers	
24	23	
25	32	
26	42	
27	21	
28	27	
29	20+20+(14)+22	
30	400	
31	6	
32	22	
33	60	2
Total =	798	2
Grand Total = 800		

The <u>sixteenth</u> checksum was with a special cycle which is known as the Sothic cycle of 1,461 years and it is shown in Table 17. It included the suspect number of 3 cubits on <u>row fifty six.</u>

Table 17: Sothic Cycle of 1,461 Years

Rows	Cubits	Treasures	
48	2	300	
49	12	80	
50		17	
51		-	
52		-	
53		-	
54		40	
55		-	
56	3	-	
57		900	
58		60	5
59		42	
	1,461 Years		

The seventeenth checksum total was with a second display with the Sothic Cycle of 1,461 years It began after the Greek letter ΣK and it included both the treasures and cubits all the way down to row thirty nine with the spur containing the indices to form Enoch's calendar as a bracket as shown in Table 18. The number 1,461 however also equated to four solar years of 1,461 days. This checksum was an indication that the numbers on the copper scroll could represent either years or days.

The eighteen checksum was with 777 + 777 or 1,554 years and it began on row forty after the spur with the indices to form Enoch's solar calendar. It include all of the cubits and treasures and ended on row fifty seven just before a spur where the ages of Enoch could be formed. The sequence is shown in Table 19 and it included the 3 cubits in column eleven which had been identified by Lefkovits. This was the second time the 3 cubits had been utilised.

Table 18: Sothic Cycle of 1,461 Years

Rows	Cubits	Treasures	
		ΣK	
16	14	55	
17	3	2	
18		200	
19		70	
20	1	12	
21	3	7	
22		No Numbers	
23	60 + 3	23	
24	7	32	
25	3	42	
26	9	21	
27	12	27	
28	9	20+20+(14)+22	
29	24	400	
30	6	6	
31	7	22	
32	3	60	2
33		a Silver Bar	
34	17	17	
35	3	7	
36	24	66	
37	11	70	
38	13	7	4
		Spur) (	
		Grand Total = 1,461	

Table 19: 777 + 777 Years

Rows	Cubits	Treasures	
38		Spur) (	
39	8.5	23.5	
40	16	22	
41		a Mina	
42	7	9	
43		No Numbers	
44		9	
45		12	
46	10	62	
47	2	300	20
48	12	80	
49		17	
50		No Numbers	
51		No Numbers	
52		No Numbers	
53		40	
54		No Numbers	
55	3	No Numbers	
56		900 Silver Talents	
57		Spur) (	
		777 + 777 or 1,554 Years	

The <u>nineteenth</u> checksum total was the equivalent of the first age of Noah at 500 years. It began on <u>row forty five</u> and included all of the treasures to <u>row fifty</u> as shown in Table 20. It was rather noticeable that the sequence began after <u>row forty four</u> which had no numbers and ended just before <u>row fifty one</u> which also had no numbers. It seemed as if the rows/sites with no numbers were a medium to form brackets.

Table 20: Noah at 500

Rows	Treasures	
44	No Numbers	
45	9	
46	12	
47	62	
48	300	20
49	80	
50	17	
51	No Numbers	
	500 Years	

The <u>twentieth</u> checksum total was with the treasures and cubits from <u>row seventeen</u> to <u>row twenty two</u> where they added up to 364 as shown in Table 21. The total of 364 compared to the number of days in Enoch's solar calendar. The sequence began after the bracket with the Greek letter

ΣK and it ended in the row before where there were no numbers. There were now several examples to indicate that the sites or rows with no numbers were intended as brackets.

Table 21: Solar Year of 364 Days

Rows	Solar Year	
	ΣK	
17	14	55
18	3	2
19		200
20		70
21	1	12
22		7
	364 Days	

The <u>twenty first</u> checksum compared to the first age of Enoch at 65 years.

Table 22: Enoch at 65

Rows	Cubits	Treasures
24	3	23
25	7	32
	65 Years	

The twenty second checksum compared to the final age of Jared at 962 years as shown in Table 23.

Table 23: Jared at 962

		42
9		21
12		27
9		76
24		400
6		6
7		22
3		60	2
		1
17		17
3		7
24		66
11		70
13		7
962 Years		

There were thus at least twenty two checksums with many of them encased within two brackets to endorse that the copper scroll was not a treasure map because it was hardly likely that the scribes would have needed to future proof the numbers if it were real treasures. For instance, would it really matter if the treasure hunters were to find 20 talents instead of 14 talents of gold or vise-versa? An overview of the checksums on the Copper Scroll is shown in Layer A below.

The checksums did their duty and the values of the missing and suspect numbers have all been determined. It stood out that there were five totals with totals of 777 which compared to the final age of Lamech and one total of 777 + 777 and these were highlighted in brown colour. Those totals with 777 were the raison d'etre of the copper scroll and they will feature in the next chapter.

Layer A: The 22 Checksums on the Copper Scroll

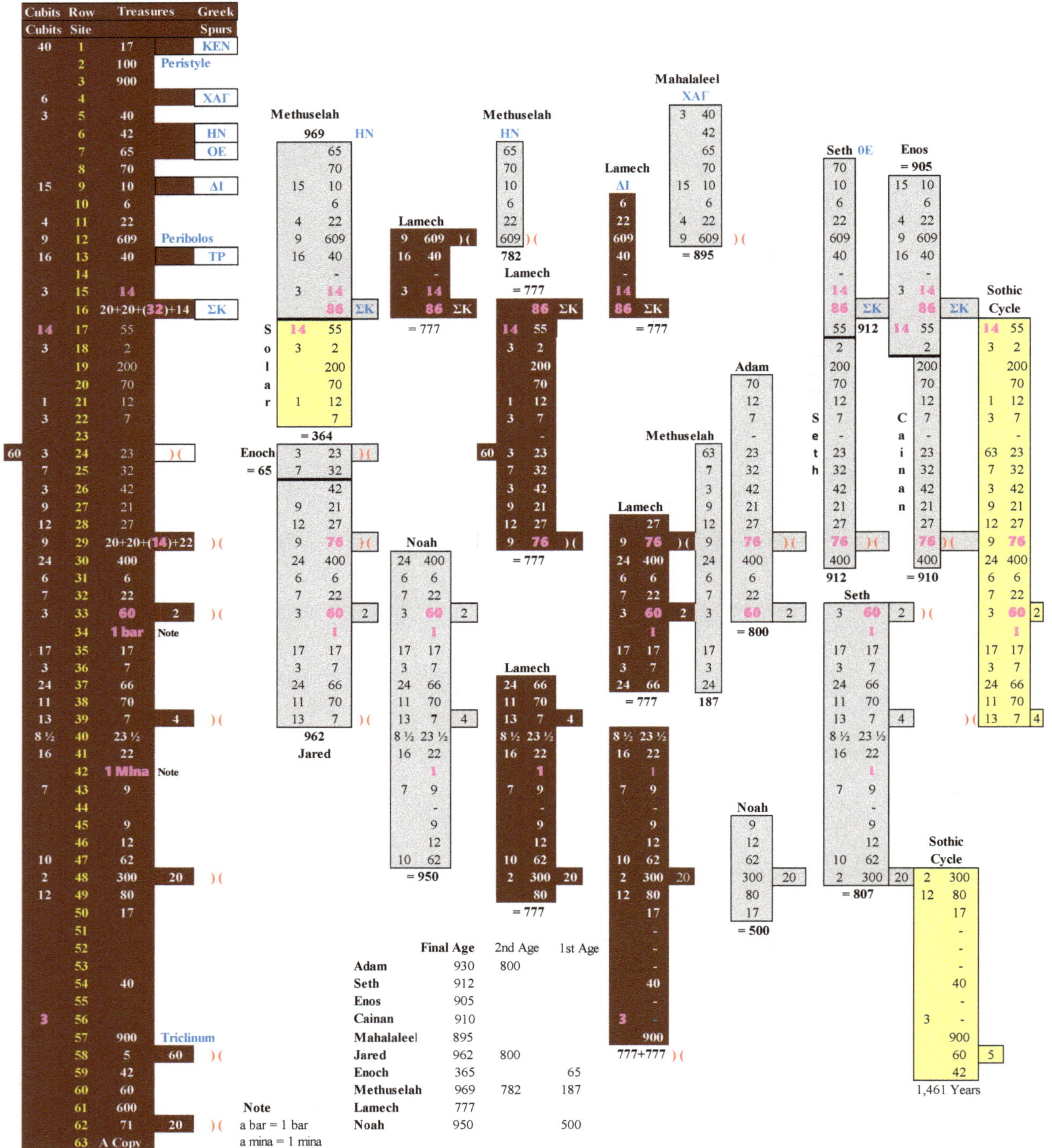

Chapter 3

The Calendar Indices on the Copper Scroll

There were five totals of 777 in the checksum exercise and they stood out as excessive. Two of those totals ran partially in parallel and that caught my attention. It was noticed that one of those totals of 777 began after the Greek loanword Peribolos where the number with 609 treasures and 9 cubits were listed on Row 12. There was a telltale sign of something peculiar where the numbers of 40 treasures and 16 cubits on Row 13 plus the 9 cubits on Row 12 added up to 65, which was the first age of Enoch. It seemed that Enoch had his arm around the number 609 and that made the number very precious.

As outlined earlier, multiplying three numbers on Row 33 to get a circle and three numbers on Row 39 to get Enoch's 364 day calendar had introduced the concept of increase and multiply. Therefore, it seemed preordained to do the same and multiply the two numbers 609 and 9 on the copper scroll. The ancient method to multiply was to add the biggest number multiple times.[5] For example, the number 609 would be added in 9 steps of which three were listed here because they equated to time periods as follows:

- Three additions of 609 at 1,827 equated to 5 solar years with 1 day of an overlap.

- Six additions of 609 at 3,654 equated to 10 solar years with 2 days of an overlap.

- Nine additions of 609 at 5,481 equated to 15 solar years with 2 days of an overlap.

The evidence suggested that the addition of 609 in nine steps was a method the scribes had employed to show that the numbers on the copper scroll represented days and could be converted to solar years.

There were seven numbers between the Greek letters of ΔI and TP where the numbers 609 and 9 were listed and these were 6, 4, 22, 9, 609, 16 and 40. This did not seem significant at first until it was detected that the numbers with 9 and 609, 4 and 22 and 16 and 40 were also encircled by the words east, west, north, and south coordinates on the copper scroll. It seemed possible that the circling of the numbers was an indication that there was a larger equation involved. The six numbers were set out as shown in Table 24.

Table 24: Six Numbers Encircled by the Coordinates East, West, North and South

Rows			Cubits	Treasures	
9	East				ΔI
10				6	
11	East		4	22	North
12	South		9	609	
13			16	40	TP
14			Western		

---

[5] O Neugebauer, Ch. 3.

A pattern soon emerged when the two numbers 4 and 22 and the numbers 16 and 40 were multiplied and the results added together for the total came to 728, which was within two days of two solar years. Step by step the pieces of a jigsaw were being exposed and therefore, the numbers were formed into an equation as shown in Table 25.

Table 25: The Equation to Form 17 Years of 6,209 Days

22×4	+	609×9	+	40×16	$= 6,209$

When multiplied and the results added together, the three sets of numbers came to a total of 6,209 and this total converted to 17 solar years when using the solar year of 365.242 days. There was the possibility of more jigsaw pieces in the puzzle because the equation with those six numbers was in the same vicinity on the copper scroll as where two of the totals with the 777 checksum modules had formed. It was therefore not a big step to realign the number 6,209 into a formation of the number 777. It formed eight listings of 777 days with 6 days of an overlap as shown in Table 26.

Table 26: Eight Periods of 777 Days

777 + 777 + 777 + 777 + 777 + 777 + 777 + 777 Days = 17 Years 7 Days

The nucleus of a 777-day yardstick to measure time seemed to be on the cards. However, while 6,209 had converted to 17 solar years, the total of eight times 777 days came to 6,216 days, which was at first glance an overlap of 7 days. To correct the error there was the number 6 between the Greek letters ΔΙ and ΤΡ but not the number 7. This anomaly took some time to figure out and the solution involved a fraction of a day. This was where 17 years multiplied out to a fraction over 6,209 days. It indicated that 17 years exactly was the real target by the scribes because intercalary days are in whole days only. It therefore would have required only 6 intercalary days to be deducted in order synchronise the count with eight periods of 777 days. The core of a unique calendar for measuring time in lots of 777 days had formed and it included the position of having intercalary days.

The outcome with 777 accounted for why there were often three or four listings of the number seven together in the Bible such as with the seven priests who walked around the walls of Jericho seven times for seven days. With Samson it was pushing the mill wheel round and round as his seven locks of hair grew back again. The imagery with those two scenes prompted of seven, seven, seven and in its tabular format of 777, that number was considered to be thoroughly divine.

The Unique 777 Day Calendar

The complete 777 day calendar timetable developed from there so it is possible to give an overview of its function and outline its indices. The purpose of the 777-day calendar was to project time into the future and it was both on earth and in the heavens. This is where an explanation is necessary about earthly and heavenly time. A year on earth is measured against a fixed point on the landscape and it is how our calendar is calibrated. It is known as the solar year and it is 365.242 days long as measured today using instrumentation. In contrast, measuring a year against a fixed star in the heavens is known as a star or sidereal year and it is 365.256 days long as measured today using instrumentation. Therefore, the sidereal year is just over twenty minutes longer than the solar year. Current opinion is that the Greek astronomer Hipparchus discovered the difference between the solar and the sidereal year around the year 127 BCE. However, before the invention of mechanical clocks around the 14th century CE, it would have been impossible to measure that tiny period of twenty minutes. But recent research by a team from the University of London published on March 12th

2021with the Amtikythera Mechanism has changed that outlook. The mechanism was found in a Roman ship that sank two thousand years ago. It was a mechanical mechanism made of tiny gear wheels and was used to predict eclipses and track the movements of the planets.[6] Therefore, our present knowledge of how advanced ancient astronomers and mechanical engineers had progressed is in need of reappraisal.

We have seen that by mapping out time in intervals of 777 days, the count reached 17 years with an overlap of six days. In my previous biblical research work on ancient calendars, I had already identified the importance of mapping out time in lots of 777 days. The breakthrough was made when I decided to carry out a simulation exercise on a calculator in counting in lots of 777 days. It was found that the count returned to almost the same day as whence the count started after 117 solar years. There were 1 ⅔ days of an overlap. This was where the analysis paid dividends because the 1 ⅔ extra days of an overlap was the difference between solar and sidereal time when projected out over the lengthy period of 117 years. (Would be one day in 72 years) It was to prove a major breakthrough because it was the first indication that biblical astronomers may have devised a method to measure out that tiny difference in time between the solar and sidereal years.

The theoretical exercise continued by projecting time in lots of 777-days and it showed that the count also returned to almost the same day as it had started after 217 years. It required adding on 3 ½ intercalary days to synchronise the count precisely with the 217 solar year period. Because history is measured in centuries of 100 years, it was decided to apply the 777 day method to measure that period. It was found that it required a fraction over five intercalary days to be added to reach 100 solar years. This multiplied out to 52 intercalary days in 1,000 solar years and just a fraction over 156 days in 3,000 solar years.

The periods of 1,000 and 3,000 years were included because they were obtained from the Book of Revelation where indices of the 777 day calendar were detected. There were six listings of one thousand years in the Book of Revelation and there were also two periods of five months and two periods of 3 ½ days. Five solar months plus 3 ½ days rounded up to 156 days, which was practically the same as the intercalary days to be added on in 3,000 years when using the 777 day method to plot out the future. (The intercalary days were 156.6 days and that figure could be rounded down to 156 days or up to 157 days) Because there were two periods of five months and also two periods of 3 ½ days in Revelation it indicated that the six listings of 1,000 years could be presented as two periods of 3,000 years at 6,000 years. The intercalary days for 6,000 solar years was thus 313 days.

The theoretical model of the 777 day method had taken on a practical dimension because it applied effectively with the two periods of 3,000 years and the two intercalary periods of 156 days in the Book of Revelation. That was as far as the research had progressed in developing the theoretical model of the 777 day calendar because it needed some backup proof to support those calculations with the time periods in the Book of Revelation. Otherwise, the exercise was open to the charge of fitting the numbers in to achieve a desired result. This was where the numbers on the copper scroll aided the development of this 777 day method for measuring time.

The next step was to take on board the difference between solar and sidereal time because it was inherent in the 117 year count with the 777-Day formula. Therefore, the theoretical simulation exercise was adjusted to cater for the sidereal year. It was found that it required six intercalary days to be added on to reach 100 sidereal years of 36,525 days when using the 777-Day formula. Those figures, including the fractions of a day projected out to 66 days to reach 1,000 sidereal years to synchronise the calendar with that period. In turn, it required 198 days to reach 3,000 sidereal years and 396 days to reach 6,000 sidereal years.

---

[6] Freeth, T., Higgon, D., Dacanalis, A. et al. A Model of the Cosmos in the ancient Greek Antikythera Mechanism. Sci Rep 11, 5821 (2021). https://doi.org/10.1038/s41598-021-84310-w.

The exercise to rebuild the 777 day calendar progressed from there by using the numbers on the copper scroll to complete the task. Most of the data concerned the totals of the treasures only or with the treasures plus the cubits between the Greek letters. To begin with, the totals of the treasures between the Greek letters ΔI and TP came to 677 while the total of the treasures between HN and ΣK came to 857. By applying the 777-day formula, the calculations identified 677 as the number of intercalary days that had to be added to synchronise the calendar with 12,960 solar years. In turn the number 857 proved to be the number of intercalary days that had to be added on to synchronise the calendar with 12,960 sidereal years. The period of 12,960 years was six constellations or the length of half a cycle of the zodiac of 25,920 years. This was a very unusual finding for the ancients were not credited with using 25,920 years as the length of the zodiac. Indeed, that figure of 25,920 years is relatively modern for it is accredited to Isaac Newton who calculated that period.

The number of treasures and cubits between the Greek letters KEN and ΔI added up to 1,251 and it compared to the 1,252 intercalary days to be added on in 24,000 solar years. Therefore, there were two numbers between sets of Greek letters, which equated to the intercalary days in 12,960 solar and sidereal years and one number that was just one day short of the intercalary days in 24,000 solar years. It was then back to the theoretical exercise and the calculations showed that the number of intercalary days for 24,000 sidereal years were 1,584 days. The period of 12,000 solar and sidereal years got bypassed by the emphasis on the role of the Greek letters, but their intercalary days were 626 and 792 days. Thereafter, it required 1,354 intercalary days and 1,711 intercalary days to be added on synchronise time with a complete cycle of the zodiac of 25,920 solar and sidereal years respectively.

At a later stage in the analysis, the periods of 200, 300, 600 and 900 years together with their intercalary days were added to the timetable. All those periods are outlined in Table 27 together with their respective intercalary days for both the solar and sidereal years. The five periods highlighted in grey at the bottom of the table will feature in the next chapter of the analysis relative to the orbits of the planets. In all the calculations, the solar year of 365.242 days and the sidereal year of 365.256 days were applied. Because some of the time periods and intercalary days had been detected between sets of Greek letters, the focus was to examine if there were the equivalent of more time periods and intercalary days between the remaining sets of Greek letters.

Table 27: The Years and Intercalary Days of a Calendar Timetable

Periods in Years	Solar Time Intercalary Days	Sidereal Time Intercalary Days
17 Years	---	---
117 Years	1 Day	0 Days
217 Years	3 Days	6 Days
100 Years	5 Days	6 Days
200 Years	11 Days	13 Days
300 Years	15 Days	20 Days
400 Years	21 Days	27 Days
600 Years	32 Days	40 Days
777 Years	40 Days	52 Days
807 Years	42 Days	53 Days
900 Years	47 Days	60 Days
1,000 Years	52 Days	66 Days
1,461 Years	76 Days	96 Days
1,554 Years	82 Days	102 Days
3,000 Years	157 Days	198 Days
6,000 Years	314 Days	396 Days
7,777 Years	406 Days	513 Days
12,000 Years	626 Days	792 Days
12,960 Years	677 Days	857 Days
24,000 Years	1,252 Days	1,584 Days
25,920 Years	1,354 Days	1,711 Days

The Calendar Periods and the Intercalary Days on the Copper Scroll

Armed with those periods and intercalary days it was plain to see that some of them were listed at the very beginning of the copper scroll as follows:

- First treasures on the scroll at 17 equated to — 17 Years
- Second treasure on the scroll at 100 equated to — 100 Years
- Both 17 and 100 added up to 117 and it equated to — 117 Years
- First three numbers on the scroll added to 157 and it equated to — 157 Days
- Total between KEN 100 + 900 XAΓ at 1,000 equated to — 1,000 Years

To form those four periods in years and one intercalary interval in days of the calendar timetable from the first four numbers on the copper scroll was an indication of what to expect in the quest. The Greek loan word *Peristyle* after the number 100 facilitated arranging the numbers in groups to form 100, 117 and, 157.

The exercise in forming time periods will now begin. Identifying those periods is not a willy nilly exercise with numbers, because the associated intercalary days for both solar and sidereal time are required to qualify that the periods were an intended part of the calendar timetable.   That was the biblical imperative of having two witnesses to justify that the periods of the timetable were legitimate.

The <u>first period</u> was 17 years and the number 17 was the first number as treasures on the copper scroll before the bracket with the Greek letters KEN. The intercalary days did not apply for 17 years because it was less than one day.

The <u>second period</u> was 100 years and it was the second number as treasures on the copper scroll and it was between the Greek letters KEN and the Greek loan word Peristyle. It was also the total of the numbers between the Greek letters TP and ΣK as shown in Table 28.

Table 28: 100 Years

Rows	Treasures
	TP
14	No Numbers
15	14
16	20+20+32+14
	ΣK
Total = 100	

- The intercalary days in 100 solar years was 5 days and the only number 5 on the scroll was on Row 58 where it was part of the equation to form two of Enoch's ages. The linkage between the two was where the number 100 was beside the number 900 on Row 3 where the treasures were buried in a sepulchral monument while the number 5 on Row 58 was also beside the number 900 on Row 57 with the treasures in a tomb.

- There were 6 intercalary days in 100 sidereal years and that numbers was on its own as 6 cubits on Row 4 between the Greek letters KEN and XAΓ where the 100 years was also listed.

The <u>third period</u> was 117 years and it was formed from the number of treasures before KEN plus the number of treasures between the Greek letters TP and ΣK as shown in Table 29.

Table 29: 117 Years

Rows	Treasures	Greek Letters
1	17	KEN
	+	
		TP
14	No Numbers	
15	14	
16	20+20+32+14	ΣK
Total = 117		

- The intercalary days for 117 solar years required one day to be subtracted. There was only one listing of the number one on the scroll and that was on Row 21 where it was shown as one cubit. There was a common feature linking 117 and its one intercalary day. On Row 1 and 2 where 117 was also formed, the treasures were buried in a sepulchral monument while the treasures on Row 21 were hidden one cubit in a burial mound.

- There was no need to look for the intercalary days in 117 sidereal years because it was zero.

The <u>fourth period</u> was 200 years and that number was listed on Row 19 as silver karsh. The intercalary days in this equation sets the trend for identifying how the scribes devised Enoch's ages and calendar indices as intercalary days.

- This period of 200 years had 11 intercalary days to be added for solar time. On Row 39 were the two numbers of 7 and 4 from Enoch's calendar indices and they added up to 11 to equate to the intercalary day for solar time.

- On the same Row 39 that was also the number 13 to cater for the 13 intercalary days in 200 sidereal years.

The <u>fifth period</u> was 217 years and the total to form that number began on Row 5 after the Greek letters ΧΑΓ and consisted of the treasures only down to Row 8 as shown in Table 30.

Table 30: 217 Years

Rows	Cubits	Treasures	Greek Letters
4	(6)		ΧΑΓ
5	(3)	40	
6		42	ΗΝ
7		65	
8		70	
Total		217	

The total started with Greek letters as a bracket but it did not end with a bracket. However, the scribes had placed its two sets of intercalary days in positions to qualify that 217 was intended. There were 3 intercalary days to be added to synchronise the calendar with 217 solar years and 6 intercalary days to be added with 217 sidereal years. This was where the positioning was commendable because the scribes had placed the number 6 in the row before where the total of 217 began and the number 3 on the row where 217 began and both were between sets of Greek letters as will be outlined.

- Three intercalary days were required to synchronise the calendar with 217 solar years and that number as 3 cubits was on its own on Row 5 between the Greek letters ΧΑΓ and ΗΝ.

- Six intercalary days were required to synchronise the calendar with 100 sidereal years and the number 6 expressed as cubits was set on its own on Row 4 between the Greek letters of ΚΕΝ and ΧΑΓ.

The trend with Enoch continued where the scribes had configured three rows of numbers to act as periods and intercalary days of the calendar timetable. Those numbers were on Rows 47, 48 and 49 of the copper scroll as outlined in Table 31.

Table 31: Rows 47, 48 and 49

Row	Cubits	Treasures	
47	10	62	
48	2	300	20
49	12	80	

Enoch was again in the limelight with this display where the number 300 was the same as his second age. The exercise to identify the calendar time periods will thus continue by using the assembly kit of numbers from the table and there will soon be many references back to this table.
The <u>sixth period</u> was 300 years and it was listed as 300 gold talents on Row 48.

- There were 15 intercalary days in 3,000 solar years and there was the number 15 cubits on its own on Row 9 between the Greek letters 0E and ΔI to cater for that requirement.

- The intercalary period for 300 sidereal years was 20 days and those two numbers were listed side by side on Row 48. It therefore, was a shop window display by the scribes with the two numbers 300 and 20 together to represent 300 sidereal years and its 20 intercalary days.

The <u>seventh period</u> was with 400 years and it compared to the 400 treasures on row thirty.

- 21 intercalary days in 400 solar years from totals of cubits at 6 between KEN and XAΓ plus 15 between OE and ΔI equals 21

- 27 intercalary days for 400 sidereal years from total of cubits between KEN and ΔI at 24 plus 3 between TP and ΣK equals 27.

The <u>eight period</u> was 600 years and that number was listed on Row 60 of the scroll as 600 gold and silver talents. But that number could also be formed by multiplying 300 by 2 on Row 48 of the scroll to get 600 and that was a magnet that led to its intercalary days..

- There were 32 intercalary days in 600 solar years. The number 32 was the total of the cubits between the Greek letters ΔI and ΣK on the scroll..

- There were 40 intercalary days in 600 sidereal years and that number was listed as 40 cubits before the Greek letters KEN

The <u>nineth period</u> was 777 years and it was formed from the treasures between ΔI and ΣK at 777.

- 40 intercalary days in 777 solar years from 40 as cubits before Greek letters KEN.

- 52 intercalary days for 777 sidereal years from total of 49 cubits on Rows 1 to 6 ending at HN plus 3 between TP and ΣK equals 52.

The <u>tenth period</u> was 807 years and it was the total of cubits and treasures from the spur on Row 33 to the spur on Row 48 at 807.

- 42 intercalary days in 807 solar years from total of 12 + 20 + 10 = 42 from Rows 47 to 49.

- 53 intercalary days in 807 sidereal years from total of cubits between KEN and TP at 53.

The <u>eleventh period</u> was 900 years and that number was on Row 57 as silver talents.

- There were 60 intercalary days in 900 sidereal years and the number 60 was listed on Row 58 immediately after the number 900. It therefore was another shop window display with the 900 years and the associated intercalary 60 days of the calendar timetable.

- There were 47 intercalary days in 900 solar years. The shop window display got bigger because there was the number 5 on Row 58 and 42 on Row 59 and they added up to 47.

It is important to point out that the translations by Puech and Lefkovits had those numbers with 900, 5, 60 and 42 all at one site or item. This can now be seen as having been pre-arranged by the scribes to serve this calendar formation with 900 years and its two sets of intercalary days. Furthermore, Puech had identified the word triclinium in the description of the site and it was an original Greek word meaning three. It was applied by the Romans in the context of three couches around a table. It would suggest that the scribes were prompting of the three calendar indices with 900, 60 and 47 with the word triclinium.

The <u>twelfth period</u> was 1,000 years and that number was formed from the number 100 on Row 2 plus 900 on Row 4 and they were between the Greek letters KEN and XAΓ.

- A total of 52 intercalary days were required to map out 1,000 solar years precisely and that total as cubits is shown in Table 32.

Table 32: 52 Intercalary Days

Rows	Cubits	Greek Letters
1	40	KEN
4	6	
5	3	
6		HN
	+	
		TP
14	No Numbers	
15	3	
16		ΣK
Total =	52	

- The number of intercalary days in 1,000 sidereal years was 66 and that number as treasures was on Row 37 of the scroll.

The <u>thirteenth period</u> was the Sothic cycle with 1,461 years and it was formed from the treasures and cubits from Row 17 after ΣK to the spur on Row 39 with total of 1,461.

- 76 intercalary days in 1,461 solar years from total of the treasures on the spur at 76 on Row 29.

- 96 intercalary days in 1,461 sidereal years from total of cubits at 96 from Row 1 to 16 ending at the Greek letters ΣK.

The <u>fourteenth period</u> was 1,554 years or 777 + 777 years and it was formed from the total of cubits and treasures at 1,554 from Row 40 after a spur to Row 57 before a spur.

- 82 intercalary days in 1,554 solar years from the treasures at 82 between XAΓ to HN.

- 102 intercalary days in 1,554 sidereal years from total of 102 treasures and cubits with 2 + 20 + 80 on Rows 48 and 49.

The <u>fifteenth period</u> was 3,000 years. That number was obtained by multiplying 300 on Row 48 by 10 from Row 47 and the total was 3,000.

- There were 157 intercalary days for 3,000 solar years and it was formed from the first three numbers on Row 1 and Row 2 on the copper scroll with 40, 17 and 100 adding up to 157. The sequence ended with a Greek loan word Peristyle as a bracket.

- The intercalary days for 3,000 sidereal years was 198 days and it was formed from the treasures and cubits from two separate combinations of the numbers, which were between the Greek letters of OE and ΔI and TP and ΣK as shown in Table 33.

Table 33: 198 Intercalary Days

Rows	Cubits	Treasures	Greek Letters
			OE
8		70	
9	15	10	ΔI
	+	+	
13			TP
14		No Numbers	
15	3	14	
16		20+20+32+14	ΣK
Totals	**18**	**180**	
Grand Total = 198			

The <u>sixteenth period</u> was 6,000 years and it was formed by multiplying 300 by 20 on Row 48 above to give the number 6,000.

- There were 314 intercalary days in 6,000 solar years and they proved to be the total of the numbers 2 + 300 + 12 = 314 on Row 48 and 49.

- The 396 intercalary days in 6,000 sidereal years were formed from 62 + 2 + 300 + 20 + 12 = 396 on Rows 47 to 49.

The <u>seventeenth period</u> was 7,777 years and it involved the multiplication of 12 cubits and 27 treasures on Row 28 and the result at 324 then multiplied by 24 from Row 30 to give 7,776 as compared to 7,776.8 for long cycle of Saturn.

- 406 intercalary days in 7,777 solar years from total of 400 plus 6 treasures on Rows 30 and 31.

- 513 intercalary days in 7,777 sidereal years from total of treasure on Row 29 plus the cubits and treasures on Rows 30 and 31 all adding to 512, which was I less than the target of 513.

The <u>eighteenth period</u> was 12,000 years and it was formed from the multiplication of 2, 300 and 20 on Row 48, which resulted with the number 12,000.

- There were 626 intercalary days required to map out 12,000 solar years and it was practically formed from the total of 609 and 16 at on Row 12 and 13 of the scroll. There total came to 625 which was a one-day error. There was a Greek loanword to act as a bracket before the number 609 and the second bracket was with the numbers that added up to Enoch's age of 65 surrounding 609 so that combination was well structured.

- There were 792 intercalary days required to synchronise the calendar with 12,000 sidereal years. A total of 791 intercalary days was formed from the addition of two separate combinations of the number of treasures and cubits between the Greek letters ΧΑΓ and ΗΝ and ΔΙ and ΤΡ as shown in Table 34.

Table 34: 791 Intercalary Days

Rows	Cubits	Treasures	Greek Letters
4			ΧΑΓ
5	3	40	
6		42	ΗΝ
	+	+	
9			ΔΙ
10		6	
11	4	22	
12	9	609	
13	16	40	ΤΡ
Totals	**32**	**759**	
Grand Total = 791			

The <u>nineteenth period</u> was 12,960 years with its six constellations of the zodiac and it proved to be the multiplication with 12 and 80 to get 960 on Row 49 plus the result from Row 48 with 12,000 to give a total of 12,960. This number equated to six constellations of the Zodiac.

- There was a linkage of 12,960 and the main formula that was between the Greek letters ΔI and TP where the period of 17 years was formed. All the four treasures in that equation added up to 677, which were the number of intercalary days in 12,960 solar years. The total was formed from the number of treasures between the Greek letters of **ΔI** and **TP** as shown in Table 35.

Table 35: 677 Intercalary Days

Rows	Treasures	Greek Letters
9		ΔI
10	6	
11	22	
12	609	
13	40	TP
Total =	677	

- A total of 857 days were required to synchronise the calendar with 12,960 sidereal years. The total was formed from the treasures between the Greek letters of OE and ΣK as shown in Table 36.

Table 36: 857 Intercalary Days

Rows	Treasures	Greek Letters
		OE
8	70	
9	10	
10	6	
11	22	
12	609	
13	40	
14	No Numbers	
15	14	
16	20+20+32+14	ΣK
Total =	857	

The <u>twentieth period</u> was 24,000 years and it required multiplying the number 300 on Row 48 by 80 on Row 49 to get 24,000.

- There were 1,252 intercalary days in 24,000 solar years and that number compared to a total of 1,251 as the number of treasures and cubits between the Greek letters KEN and ΔI as shown in Table 37.

Table 37: 1,251 Intercalary Days

Rows	Cubits	Treasures	Greek Letters
1			KEN
2		100	
3		900	
4	6	No Numbers	
5	3	40	
6		42	
7		65	
8		70	
9	15	10	ΔI
Totals	**24**	**1,227**	
Grand Total = 1,251			

- total of 1,584 intercalary days were required to map out 24,000 sidereal years precisely. The intercalary days for 1,000 sidereal years had been outlined earlier where it was listed as 66 talents on Row 37 of the Copper Scroll. The scribes had again showed their ingenuity where they listed 24 cubits with the 66 talents because the two numbers multiplied out to 1,584 and this was the same as the number of intercalary days in 24,000 sidereal years. By using the old method of 24 additions of 66, it meant that the intercalary days would be displayed for each of the one-thousand-year periods beginning at 1,000 years and ending at 24,000 years.

The <u>twenty first period</u> was one cycle of the zodiac at 25,920 years and it required multiplying the earlier result of 12,960 by 2 from Row 48 to get 25,920 years.

- A total of 1,354 intercalary days were required to synchronise the calendar with one cycle of the zodiac of 25,920 solar years. The total was formed from the numbers of treasures and cubits between the Greek letters of KEN and ΔI plus the numbers between TP and ΣK as shown in Table 38.

Table 38: 1.354 Intercalary Days

Rows	Cubits	Treasures	Greek Letters
			KEN
2		100	
3		900	
4	6	No Numbers	
5	3	40	
6		42	
7		65	
8		70	
9	15	10	ΔI
	+	+	
			TP
14		No Numbers	
15	3	14	
16		20+20+32+14	ΣK
Totals	**27**	**1,327**	
Grand Total = 1,354			

- The total of 1,711 days was required to synchronise the calendar with one cycle of the zodiac at 25,920 sidereal years. In comparison, a total of 1,712 was formed from the numbers of treasures and cubits between the Greek letters of KEN and XAΓ plus the numbers between ΔI and TP as shown in Table 39.

Table 39: 1,711 Intercalary Days

Rows	Cubits	Treasures	Greek Letters
1			KEN
2		100	
3		900	
4	6	No Numbers	XAΓ
	+	+	
9			ΔI
10		6	
11	4	22	
12	9	609	
13	16	40	TP
Totals	**35**	**1,677**	
Grand Total = 1,712			

Thus, twenty one periods had been identified and nineteen of them were qualified by the biblical imperative of two witnesses, where each of them had the associated intercalary days for both solar and sidereal time. The period of 117 years only required the solar intercalary days as it had zero leap days in sidereal time. The first period with 17 years was too small to have intercalary days. The intercalary days were the concrete evidence of two witnesses to verify the legitimacy of the long term time periods. It was a feat of genius by the scribes how the 19 intercalary days had been configured between the Greek letters or combinations thereof as shown in Layer B of the copper scroll. The intercalary days are shown in cream colour and they show that the Greek letters and loanwords on the copper scroll were to act as brackets to form the numbers into groups.

Layer B: 19 Intercalary Days between the Greek Letters and Loanwords on the Copper Scroll

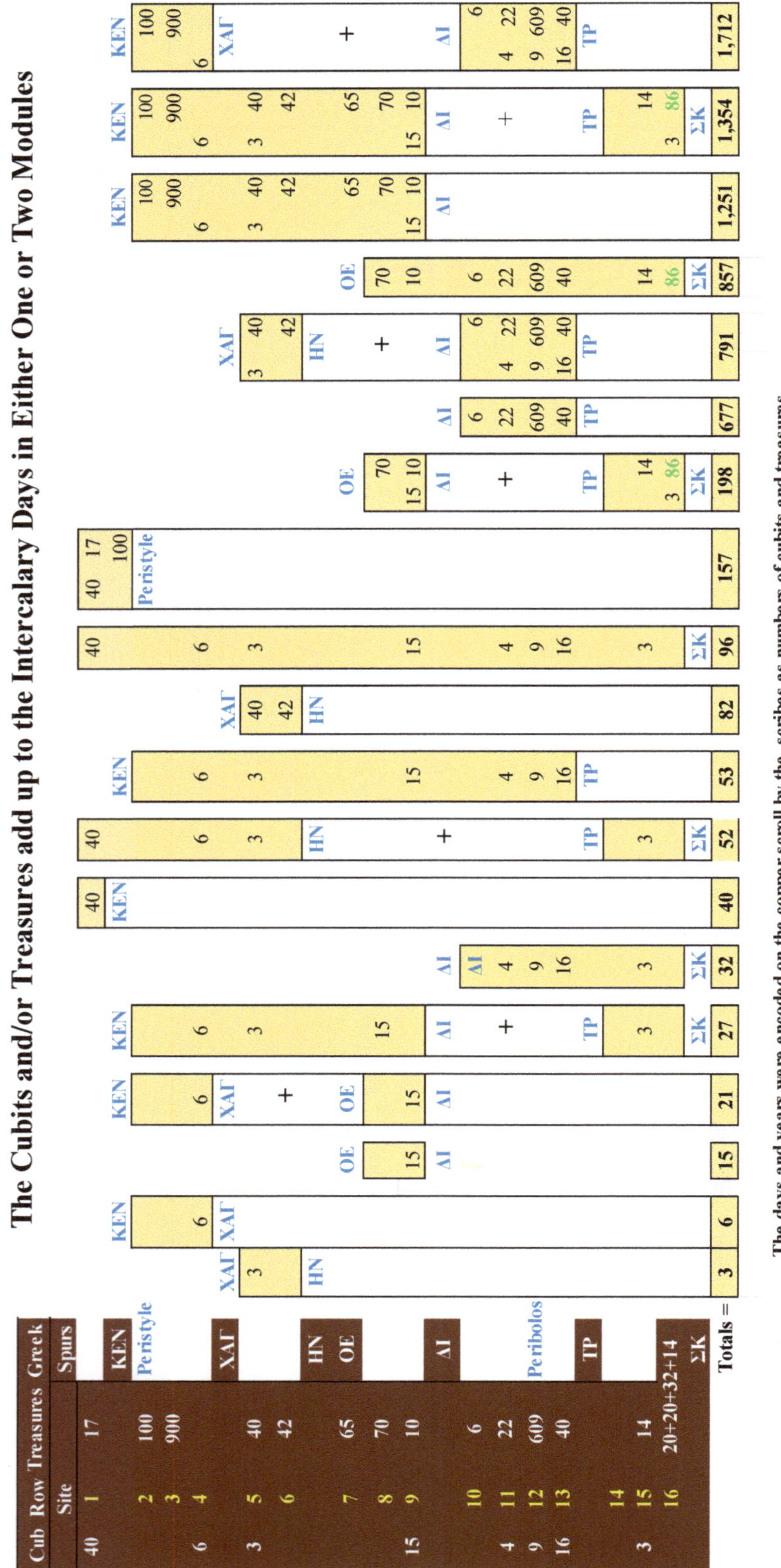

- On Rows 1 to 16 are nineteen of the intercalary days in vertical modular format highlighted in cream colour. There are twelve single modules of intercalary days and seven groups with two modules each. All of the numbers added up in sequence between sets of Greek letters and one Greek loanword.

- There was the assembly kit of numbers that formed the period of 17 years and also eight times 777 between the Greek letters ΔI and TP as was outlined earlier.

Those time periods and intercalary days between the sets of Greek letters were there by design and should satisfy even the most ardent sceptic. But there may still be a doubting Thomas that refuses to accept the result saying that the figures were rigged. With that in mind, a litmus test was carried out with the numbers between the Greek letters. The Greek letters retained their positions but the positions of the existing numbers were chosen at random with the rows or sites they would occupy. The test then was to see how many of the calendar indices could be formed from the totals of the numbers between the Greek letters in the new layout. At that stage in the research, there were a total of 14 calendar indices with years and intercalary days.

This exercise was carried out and in the new layout position with the numbers, only five of the calendar indices could be formed from the totals of the cubits and/or treasures between the Greek letters as compared to fourteen indices from the original layout. But there was more for the equation involving the numbers 609 and 9 and their surrounding numbers of 4, 22, 16, and 40 could not readily be carried out because those six numbers were now all scattered throughout the rows. Indeed, it would take a gross manipulation with those six numbers to try and relate them together so as to perform the equation to get 17 years and eight times the number 777. Therefore, the test clearly proved that the original layout of the numbers between the Greek letters was deliberately designed to house fourteen of the calendar indices and to lay the format to perform the equation to get 17 years with its eight periods of 777 days.

Measuring with a Reed

When forming the checksums, five sequences added up to 777 and one sequence added up to 777 + 777 making a total of seven times the number 777. The timetable showed that the 777-Day formula was the yardstick for mapping out time into the future. Therefore, it was time to give this 777 day calendar method a name. There were several references in the Bible to measuring with a reed the first of which was in the Book of Ezekiel. (Ezekiel 40:3) Several more references were in the Book of Revelation and the findings that have been outlined suggested that the reed was the name of the 777 day method of measuring time. (Revelation 11:1, 22:15, 16) Therefore, this method of measuring time in intervals of 777 days was named the Reed 777-Day formula.

Chapter 4

The Copper Scroll Tree of Celestial Knowledge

You may be wondering what was the purpose of those time periods with their intercalary days? It was to overcome chaos. The ancients lived beneath the stars and life revolved around them. The planet roved around in the night sky with the moon every month while the seasons followed the sun. A hunters life was aided by the moon while farmers depended on the sun to sow their crops in order to expect plenitude at harvest time. Over the years, the time keeping watchers would have plotted out the cycles of the seasons together with the luminaries using numbers to record their observations. Along the way, numbers became supreme and by using them it proved possible to predict the cycles of the solar year and those of the luminaries.

It was one day at a time in the classroom until intervals of 111 days developed into counting and then into intervals of 777 days. The natural cycles of the sun, moon and stars were imperfect because time was always going out of synchronisation with itself. A 365 day solar year without the corrective leap day every four years saw the calendar fall a month behind in the period of 120 years. That eventually led to the Sothic cycle where the seasons returned to normal after 1,461 years. It was a very long period in time and it is attributed to the lengthy dynasty of the Egyptians who stuck rigidly to a 365 day solar year. To achieve perfection and avoid such chaos, the biblical watchers factored in the additions of intercalary leap days into the recording system.

Mercury

The orbit of Mercury is 87.95 days long and it is usually rounded up to 88 days. Its long term cycle is seven years or 2,556 days and also 46 years. The configuration with the orbit of Mercury was with the treasures from Row 31 to 33 and the total was 88 and its long-term cycle of 46 years was with the treasures and cubits on the same rows as shown in Table 40. The long-term cycle of 2,556 days with Mercury will feature in the main spreadsheet shortly.

Table 40: Orbit and Cycle of Mercury

Rows	Treasures
31	6
32	22
33	60
	88 Days

Rows	Cubits	Treasures
31	6	6
32	7	22
33	3	2
	46 Years	

Venus

The orbit of Venus is 224.7 days and its long-term anniversary is eight years or 2,920 days and 777 years. The configuration with the orbit of Venus was with the treasures only from Row 33 to 39 and the total was 225 while the long-term cycle of Venus at 777 years with the treasures from Row 9 to Row 16 as shown on Table 41. The long term cycle of Venus at 2,920 days will feature in the main spreadsheet shortly.

Table 41: Orbit and Cycle of Venus

Rows	Treasures
33	60
34	1
35	17
36	7
37	66
38	70
39	4
225 Days	

Rows	Treasures
9	ΔI
10	6
11	22
12	609
13	40
14	No Numbers
15	14
16	20+20+32+14
	ΣK
777 Years	

The Lunar and Solar Year

The lunar year consists of twelve lunar months and it is 354.35 days long. The configuration with the lunar year was detected and it began on Row 33 with a spur but it only included the 60 treasures on that row. It continued down to the treasures only on Row 41 and the total was 354, which was the equivalent of the lunar year. The configuration is shown in Table 42.

Enoch's Solar calendar was 364 days long and it consisted of the cubits and treasures from Row 17 to Row 22 as shown in Table 43. The sequence began after the Greek letters ΣK.

Table 42: Lunar Year   Table 43: Solar Year

Rows	Lunar Year	
33		60
34		1
35	17	17
36	3	7
37	24	66
38	11	70
39	13	7
40	8 ½	23 ½
41		22
354 Days		

Rows	Solar Year	
	ΣK	
17	14	55
18	3	2
19		200
20		70
21	1	12
22		7
364 Days		

Mars

The orbit of Mars at 687 days and its long-term cycles are 79, 158 and 395 years are shown in Table 44 below.

Table 44: Orbit and Three Cycles of Mars

Rows	Treasures
9	10
10	6
11	22
12	609
13	40
687 Days	

Rows	Cubits	Treasures
12	9	
13	16	40
14		
15		14
79 Years		

Rows	Cubits	Treasures
16		86
17	14	55
18	3	
158 Years		

Rows	Cubits	Treasures
17	14	
18	3	2
19		200
20		70
21	**1**	12
22	3	7
23		
24	60	23
395 Years		

Jupiter

The analysis then focused on Jupiter whose orbit is 4,332.59 days long and its long-term cycles are 344, 688 and 1,554 years. The orbit of Jupiter will feature in the main spreadsheet. It was found that all of the treasures from Row 17 to Row 20 added up to 344, which compared to the long-term cycle of Jupiter at 344 years as shown in Table 45. The total of the cubits and treasures from Row 12 to 15 added up to 688, which compared to the long-term cycle of Jupiter at 688 years as shown in Table 46. The long-term cycle of Jupiter at 777 + 777 years or 1,554 years consisted of the cubits and treasures from Row 40 to Row 57 as shown in Table 47.

Table 45: Cycle of Jupiter at 344 Years.   Table 46: Cycle of Jupiter at 688 Years

Rows	Cubits	Treasures
17	14	55
18	3	2
19		200
20		70
		344 Years

Rows	Cubits	Treasures
12	9	609
13	16	40
14		
15		14
		688 Years

Table 47: Cycle of Jupiter at 777 + 777 Years

Rows	Cubits	Treasures
		Spur) (
40	8.5	23.5
41	16	22
42		a Mina
43	7	9
44		No Numbers
45		9
46		12
47	10	62
48	2	300
49	12	80
50		17
51		No Numbers
52		No Numbers
53		No Numbers
54		40
55		No Numbers
56	3	No Numbers
57		900
		Spur) (
		777 + 777 Years

(Row 48: 20)

Saturn

The orbit of Saturn is 10,759 days long and its long-term cycles are 324, 707 and 7,777 years. The long-term cycle of 324 years is shown on Table 48 and 707 years on Table 49.

Table 48: Cycle of Saturn 324 Years   Table 49: Cycle of Saturn 707 Years

Rows	Cubits	Treasures
24	63	23
25	7	32
26	2	42
27	9	21
28	12	27
29	9	76
		324 Years

Rows	Treasures
13	40
14	
15	14
16	86
17	55
18	2
19	200
20	70
21	12
22	7
23	
24	23
25	32
26	42
27	21
28	27
29	76
	707 Years

As the analysis progressed, the orbits of each planet and several of the long-term years were entered into individual stand-alone tables as was outlined so far. With so many tables with the planets, it became essential to see how they were distributed on a spreadsheet copy of the copper scroll. It was a revelation because a picture materialised with each planet and their long-term cycles as they were drawn in their fixed positions relative to where their numbers were on the scroll. That picture formed into the shape of a tree with a trunk laden with the numbers of cubits and treasures in the centre and the tables and the orbits of the planets and their long-term cycles evenly distributed like branches on the trunk. Some of the translators of the copper scroll had identified two tamarisk trees in column four and they were evergreen trees, which symbolised perseverance, longevity and eternal life. Abraham planted a tamarisk tree in a covenant with a king and it was viewed by biblical commentators as passing on the baton to future generations. (Genesis 12:1-3, 21:33) This bore a similarity with what the scribes had done with this tree of celestial knowledge where they preserved it on endurable copper to pass it onto future generations.

The tables with the planets and their long-term cycles are displayed in the picture overleaf and it speaks a thousand words. To form those tables, all of the numbers were in sequences and they included the cubits and treasures or just the treasures only. Some modules began with just the cubits or treasures while others ended in like manner. The key to understand the code was that the numbers paraded as cubits and treasures were actually neutral numbers, which could be applied as days, years or recognisable totals. It was only a matter of adding up the numbers to get the totals with the orbits and long-term cycles of the planets. The orbits are shown in dark green colour and there were two displays with Venus. The long-term cycles for the planets are shown in light green. Each planet name is highlighted with particular colours.

The time has come for the reader to participate in the adventure. Instead of perspiring laboriously with spades in humid arid terrain digging to find suspect buried treasures, your task is pleasantly exciting. Just like looking for the departure gate at an airport, follow the row numbers down the spreadsheet until you reach the row where the planet is highlighted. Then check and ensure that the numbers in the table which were paraded as cubits and treasures, add up in sequence to totals that compare with the days or years with the particular planet. Continue the adventure by finding the rows to locate each of the planets and note how many of the tables were between or started and ended with Greek letters or loanwords and the spurs.

Mercury in pink colour text: Go to Rows 31 to 33 and check that the numbers of treasures in sequence added up to 88 which compared to the orbit of Mercury at 88 days. See how its long-term cycle of 46 years compared to the total of cubits and treasures in sequence in the same rows.
Check that the cubits and treasures from Row 24 to Row 57 add up to 2,559 which compared to the long-term cycle of Mercury at 2,557 days.

Venus in blue colour text: Next go to Rows 33 to 39 and check that the treasures in sequence added up to 225 which compared to the orbit of Venus at 225 days.
The treasures from Row 30 to Row 61 added up to 2,924 ½, which compared to the long-term cycle of Venus at 2,921 Days.
Consider the treasures and cubits in Row 16 and Row 29 as a group because they had plus signs between their numbers while the cubits on Row 24 had an implied plus sign. It was pre-arranged how those three sets of numbers added up to the same total as orbit of Venus at 225 days.

See how the cubits and treasures from Row 16 to 29 added up to the total of 777, which as years proved to be a long-term cycle of Venus. This configuration with Venus and 777 years was shaped by the spurs on Rows 16, 24 and 29 and visually, it looked like the Paleo-Hebrew letter he or H.

Lunar Year in black colour: Next are Rows 33 to 41 where the cubits and treasures in sequence totalled 354, which compared to the number of days in the lunar year.

Solar Year in black colour text: Then see how the cubits and treasures on Rows 17 to 22 added up to 364, which compared to the number of days in the biblical solar year.

Mars in brown colour text: Check that the treasures in sequence from Row 9 to 13 add up to 687, which compared to the orbit of Mars. The total of the cubits and treasures in the table from Row 12 to Row 15 compared to the long-term cycles of Mars at 79 years.

Jupiter in purple colour text: Check that the treasures from Row 12 to Row 62 added up to 4,331 ½, which compared to the orbit of Jupiter at 4,332.59 days.
Running in parallel with the orbit of Jupiter were two of its long-term cycles on the copper scroll. The total of the cubits and treasures from Row 17 to Row 20 at 344 compared to the long-term cycle of Jupiter at 344 years. The long-term cycle of Jupiter at 777 + 777 or 1,554 years was further down the copper scroll. This last period was rather sensational because there were 131 cycles of Jupiter's orbit of 4,332.59 days in 777 + 777 or 1,554 years. The mystery of the number 777 had intrigued biblical devotees for centuries but it took the copper scroll to reveal it had a cosmic halo with the orbits of Jupiter and also in the earlier display with Venus.

Layer C: The Tree of Celestial knowledge on the Copper Scroll

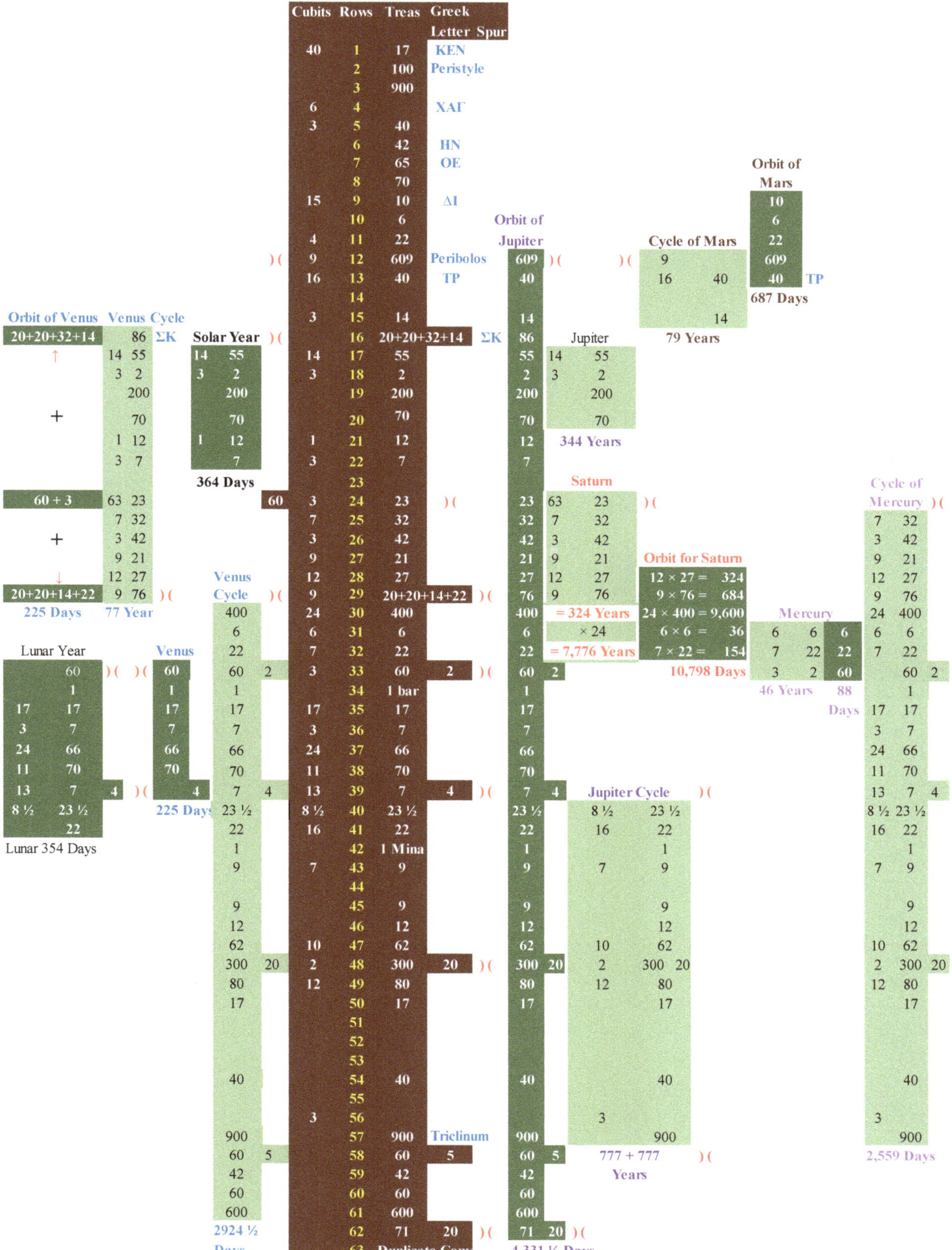

Saturn in red colour text: Check the multiplications of the treasures and cubits on Rows 28 to 32 and their subsequent additions to ensure the total came to 10,798 as compared to 10,759 days for the orbit of Saturn. But was there a quirk in the equation? For instance, four of the treasures were with weights while one was with six silver bars. The total of the computation with the weights came to 10,762, which was three days longer than the orbit of Saturn. To support this position, there was a listing of the words 4 sides in the text on Row 30 and it seemed like a prompt that four weights only were to be applied and not the six bars.

On Rows 24 to 29 the total of the cubits and treasures added up to 324, which compared to 324 years for the long-term cycle of Saturn. In turn, the multiplication of 324 years by 24 from Row 30, the total at 7,776 compared to the long-term cycle of Saturn at 7,776.83 years.

That completes the demonstration with the orbits and long-term cycles of the planets and how the scribes configured the tables of astronomy on top of the timetable and the checksums is a mystery, which will open many a mind about the presence of a superintelligence back in antiquity.

The Long-term Cycles of the Planets on a Babylonian Tablet

The long-term cycles of featured with all of the planets that the ancients could see and it was therefore, prudent to check if there was evidence of them in antiquity. It was found that there were recordings of those long-term anniversary periods where they were written on Babylonian tablets dating back to the 4th century BCE. The tablets had listings of those periods with Venus, Mars and Jupiter together with various long periods for Mercury and Saturn. The simulation exercise was therefore on a firm footing and because the Jews were exiled in Babylon, it indicated that it may have been there the biblical writers had acquired that knowledge. The researcher of the Babylonian tablet had called those long-term time periods *"Goal Years."*[7]

The Book of Judas

In the investigation, the Book of Judas was referenced and it told how Jesus taught Judas about cosmology and he referred to the stars bringing matters to completion. The gospel outlined how each of the five stars who ruled over the underworld had the names of angels. Jesus referred to a star named Sarkas completing the span of time assigned to him. It also inferred that the other remaining stars may have had particular time spans. The chapter finished with Judas asking Jesus why he was laughing at us. Jesus answered as follows: *"I am not laughing at you but at the error of the stars, because those six stars wander about with these five combatants, and they all will be destroyed along with their creatures."*

This reference to the six wandering stars was outlined by the translator in a footnote where he named them as probably Mercury, Venus, Mars, Jupiter and Saturn along with the moon. That fitted in with these findings where the orbits of five planets and the moon were found on the copper scroll. The gospel had also referred to a span of time for the star named Sarkas and to five combatants. Those five combatants were the likely candidates to be the time spans of when those wandering stars came in out of the abyss of the underworld darkness on each of their special anniversaries. And appropriately, there were only five of the special anniversaries because the moon and Venus shared the same anniversary in periods of eight years.

The Gospel of Judas was only discovered in recent times and its contents were questioned especially as Judas was shown to have been chosen by Jesus to betray him to the high priest. But we can now see from the references to the errors of the six wandering stars, that the author was on the

---

[7] Herman Hunger, p 202 – 205.

inside track of the secret knowledge of the heavens. Therefore, at least that part of the gospel of Judas was more revealing than the four official gospels.

The Magical Configurations with 7, 777, 777 + 777, 7,777 Years and 777 × 777 Days.

The track record with seven's was astonishing with periods of 7 years, 777 years, 777 + 777 years and 7,777 years. It went even further where three cycles of the zodiac came to 77,760 years, which was just 17 years short of 77,777 years. Did the biblical timekeepers consider each constellation to be 2,160.47 years long for it would have resulted with 77,777 years for three cycles of the zodiac? There was an additional period and it was 777 days by 777 times, which was a period of 1,653 years to within seventeen intercalary days. The scribes had structured those five long-term cycles to run in parallel as shown in Table 50.

Table 50: The Periods of 7 Years, 777 Years, 777 + 777 Years, 777 × 777 Days, 7,777 Years.

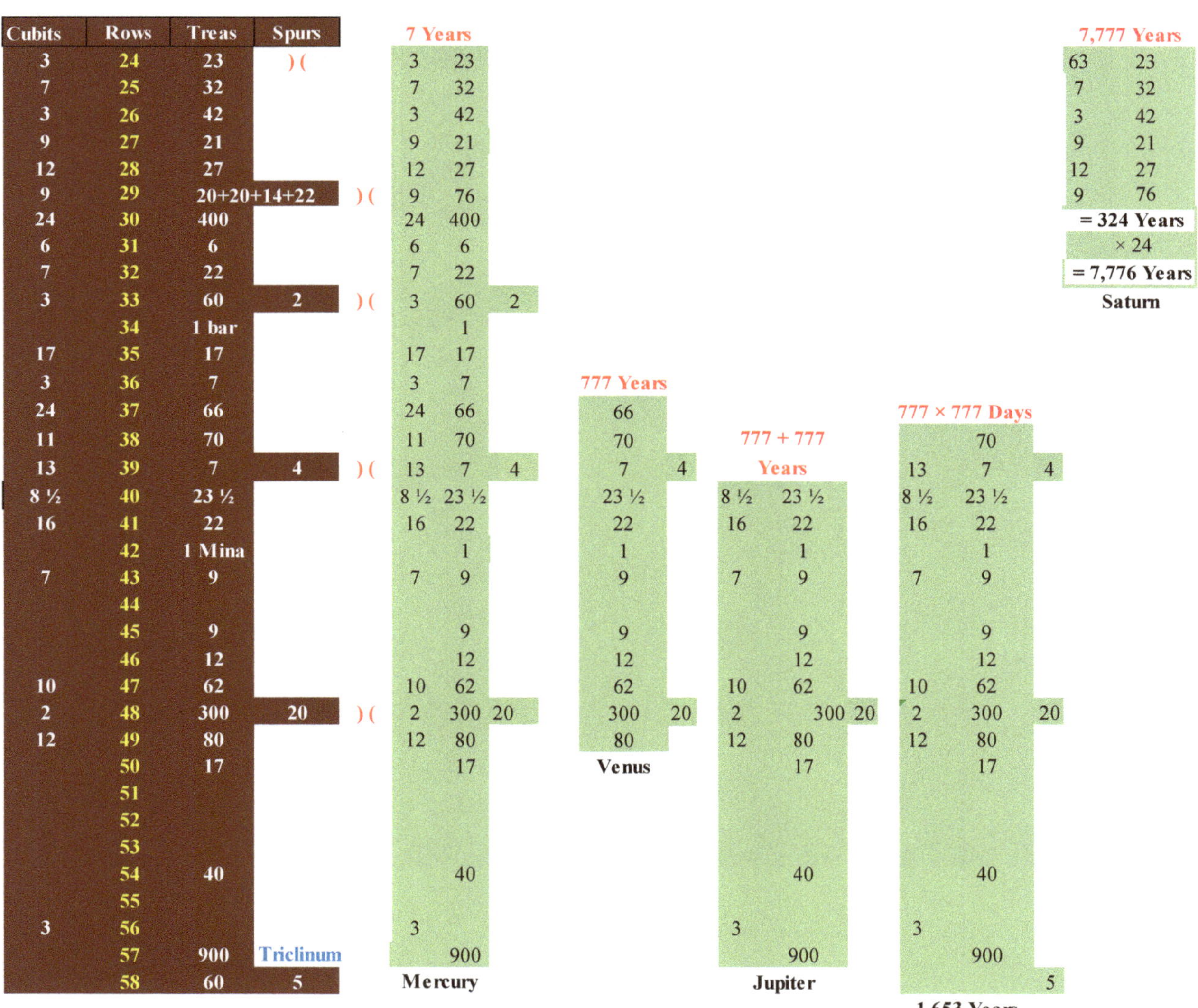

Cubits	Rows	Treas	Spurs	
3	24	23		)(
7	25	32		
3	26	42		
9	27	21		
12	28	27		
9	29	20+20+14+22		)(
24	30	400		
6	31	6		
7	32	22		
3	33	60	2	)(
	34	1 bar		
17	35	17		
3	36	7		
24	37	66		
11	38	70		
13	39	7	4	)(
8 ½	40	23 ½		
16	41	22		
	42	1 Mina		
7	43	9		
	44			
	45	9		
	46	12		
10	47	62		
2	48	300	20	)(
12	49	80		
	50	17		
	51			
	52			
	53			
	54	40		
	55			
3	56			
	57	900	Triclinum	
	58	60	5	

The celestial view of the long-term cycles with all the sevens is shown in the image below.

The Magical Configurations with the Cycles of the Planets

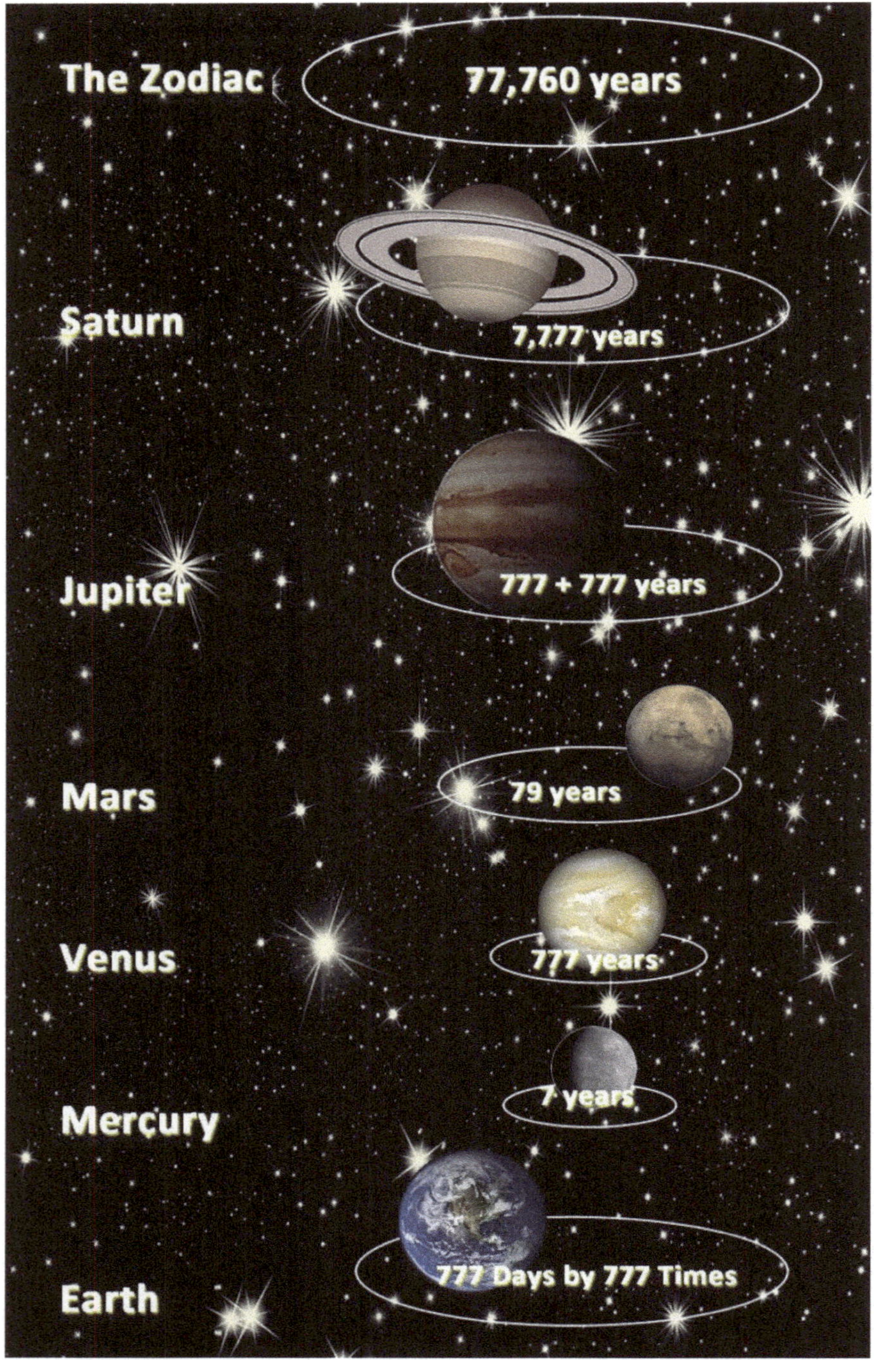

Chapter 5

The Image of a Cross on the Copper Scroll

Every jigsaw game comes in a box with the big picture on the cover so that the child can piece all of the parts together by adhering to the guiding image. But there was no such image accompanying the copper scroll to guide us on how to place the pieces together and form an intended picture. The scribes however, had prepared the way in the layout where they had programmed in the periods of the 777-day calendar in strategic positions on the copper scroll. By joining the dots together, the big picture that materialised was in the majestic shape of a cross.

The upright stem of a cross was partially formed by the five listings of the numbers 777 and twice that period with 777 + 777, which ran like a spine down the copper scroll from Row 10 to Row 57. The eight times the number 777 in 17 years as was shown in Table 24 were formed from the numbers on Rows 10 to 13 of the copper scroll and they were positioned in the exact place where the beam of a cross would be situated. Encircling those same numbers were the east, western, north and south coordinates and this introduced the concept of a solar cross. The solar cross is formed where a sundials shadow from the sun traces out a cross on the landscape with the north, south, east and west coordinates in accord with the seasons. A sundial was found at Qumran.

The short upright stem at the top of the cross was formed from the numbers of the timetable beginning at Row 1 with 17 and followed by 100 and then 1,000 and followed by the sequence with the total of number 217 from Row 5 down to Row 8 of the copper scroll. Then came the assembly kit of numbers with eight times 777 day in 17 years from Rows 10 to 13. The long stem of the cross was with five times 777 and twice that period with 777 + 777 from Rows 10 to 57 on the copper scroll as shown in the image below.

The picture of a cross took on a ghostly profile when it was found that it featured with the translator John Allegro when he deciphered the copper scroll. This was referred to by Puech where at Site 44 of the copper scroll, he had a footnote, which read as follows: *"I cannot see where, in this column (first column of the small scroll), Allegro has managed to find confirmation of a crucifixion: "In the sepulchre of the Son of Sleep, the Crucified (or Hanged)"; cf. Davies (2002:30-32)."*[8] How did Allegro decipher that statement about a crucifixion? To add substance to allegro's statement about a crucifixion, there were the east, south, north and west coordinates on that part of the copper scroll thus signalling another shape of a cross.

---

[8] Puech 2015, p. 75.

The Image of a Cross on the Copper Scroll

Cubit	Row	Treasures	Greek
		Site	
40	1	17	KEN
	2	100	Peristyle
	3	900	
6	4		ΧΑΓ
3	5	40	
	6	42	HN
	7	65	OE
	8	70	
15	9	10	ΔΙ
	10	6	
4	11	22	
9	12	609	Peribolos
16	13	40	TP
	14		
3	15	14	
	16	20+20+32+14	ΣΚ
14	17	55	
3	18	2	
	19	200	
	20	70	
1	21	12	
3	22	7	
	23		
3	24	23	
7	25	32	
3	26	42	
9	27	21	
12	28	27	
9	29	20+20+14+22	
24	30	400	
6	31	6	
7	32	22	
3	33	60	2)(
	34	a bar	
17	35	17	
3	36	7	
24	37	66	
11	38	70	
13	39	7	4)(
8 ½	40	23 ½	
16	41	22	
	42	a Mina	
7	43	9	
	44		
	45	9	
	46	12	
10	47	62	
2	48	300	20)(
12	49	80	
	50	17	
	51		
	52		
	53		
	54	40	
	55		
3	56		
	57	900	Triclinum
	58	5	60)(
	59	42	
	60	60	
	61	600	
	62	71	20)(
	63	A Copy	

(Left margin marker: **60**)

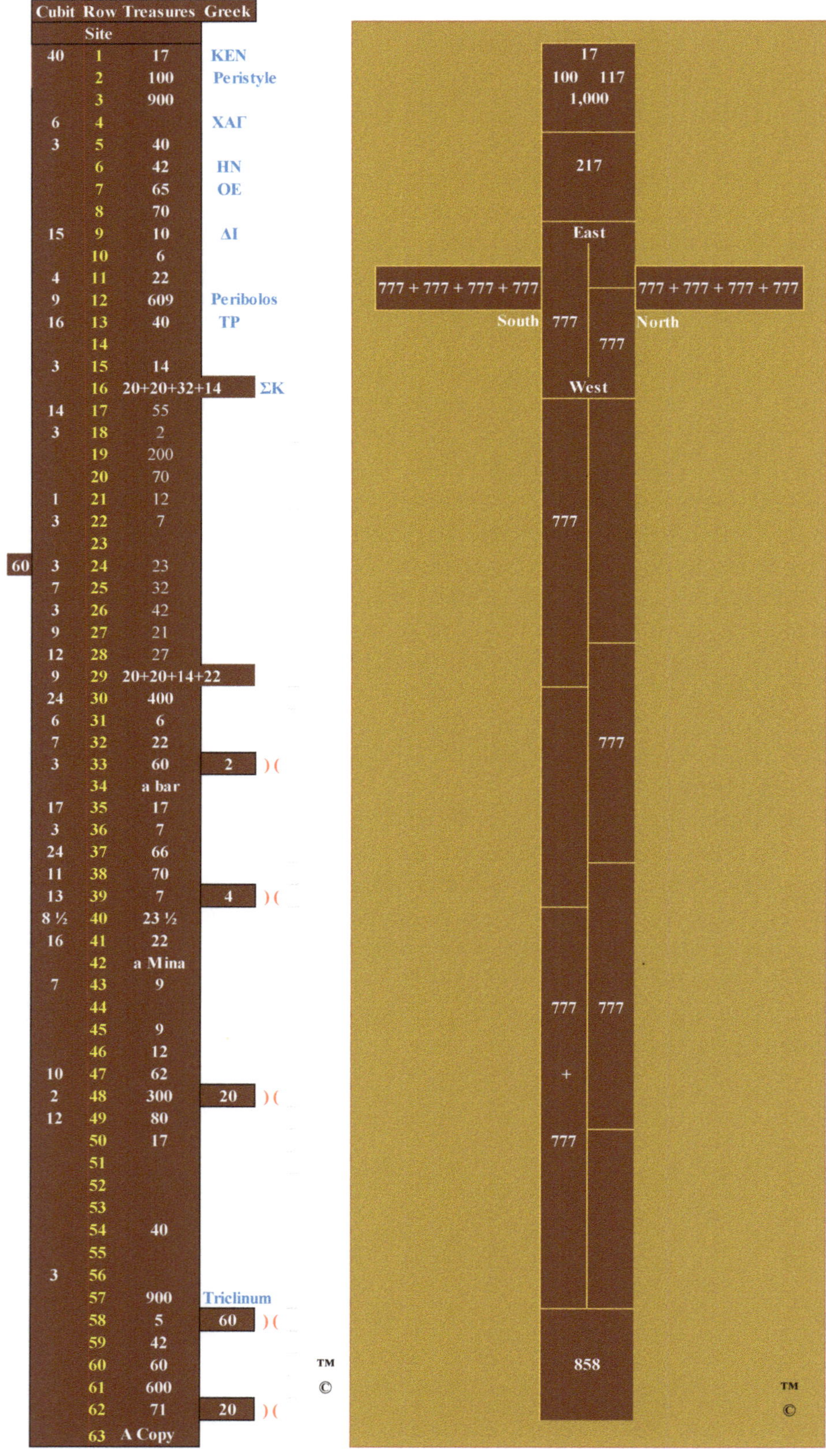

Chapter 6

The Divine Autograph of YHWH on the Copper Scroll

It was detected that some of the modular configurations with the number 777 and the planets also looked similar to letters in the Paleo Hebrew alphabet. The observation about their resemblance was only noticed long after the illustrations were drawn. It therefore was necessary to apply great attention to detail when drawing the illustrations in case the scribes had included elements that aided the formations of the Paleo Hebrew letters. The configuration with those tables and illustrations formed naturally as the numbers from the copper scroll were applied. It was only then that the symbols such as the Greek letters and the spurs with the extra treasures at some sites took on another significance than just forming brackets. They were at pivotal positions to form the boughs for the branches of the Celestial Tree of Knowledge and now they also seemed to play a role where the spurs made the illustrations look like some of the Paleo Hebrew letters.

All through the analysis of the data on the copper scroll, the conventional way of writing from left to right was applied. However, the observation with the similarity with the Paleo Hebrew letters, it required the writing and diagrams to be applied from right to left in accord with the Hebrew method of writing. Therefore, for this part of the analysis, the entries on the tables will be from right to left with the cubits first followed by the treasures. The letters that developed into the Paleo-Hebrew alphabet were a series of pictograms that began with an ox head for the letter Aleph or A. That form of early writing was used by the Israelites and can be traced back to around 1,000 BCE. Paleo-Hebrew letters continued to be used long after the Masoretic square shaped alphabet was introduced around the time of the exile in 500 BCE. The important feature for the forthcoming analysis was the pictorial displays because they were illustrations of natural everyday forms of observation. The major difference was that the scribes of the copper scroll created the images of the Paleo-Hebrew letters from their records of the orbits and long-term cycles of the planets. In essence, the ensuing words were written in the stars.

There were extra treasures on Rows 16, 29, 33, 39, 48 and 58 and spurs had to be drawn on the spreadsheet to cater for the extra numbers. It was similar on Row 23 where a spur catered for extra cubits. It became obvious that these spurs were deliberately designed to add arms or legs to the tables of figures so that they symbolised particular letters in the Paleo-Hebrew alphabet. Therefore, the tables were upgraded to pictorial illustrations in the analysis.

There were two illustrations which resembled the Paleo-Hebrew letter *he* ⅃ with H as its English display and also two separate configurations that were similar to Paleo-Hebrew letter Wah Y with its English display of W. The third configuration was where the illustration resembled the Paleo-Hebrew letter Yod ⅂ with its English display Y. Those Paleo-Hebrew spelled out the divine name YHWH when presented from right to left as follows:

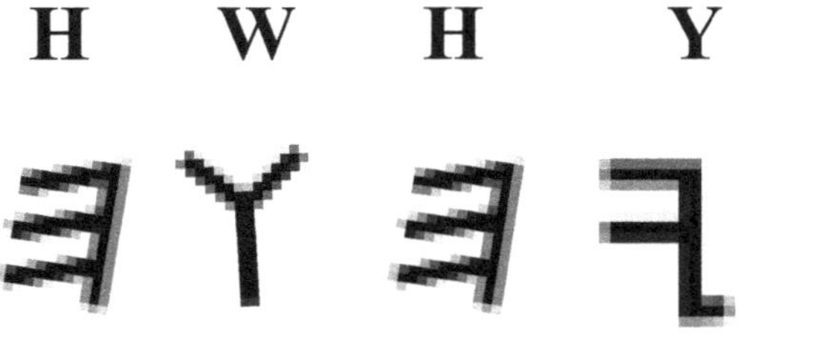

[9]

The various configurations which resembled the Paleo-Hebrew letters will now be outlined.

The first module was with the orbit of Venus at 225 days and its long-term cycle at 777 years as shown in Illustration 1. The numbers in the three spurs stretched out like three arms and their combined total came to 225, which compared to the orbit of Venus. In turn, the total of the cubits and treasures in sequence from Row 16 to Row 29 added up to 777, which compared to the long-term cycle of Venus at 777 years. The totals of the numbers on Rows 16, 24 and 29 are shown because it made the column slimer. The modular version is shown alongside the Paleo-Hebrew letter, which is known as *he* or H in the English language.

Illustration 1:

The Orbit of Venus and 777 Years   Modular Display with Letter *he*

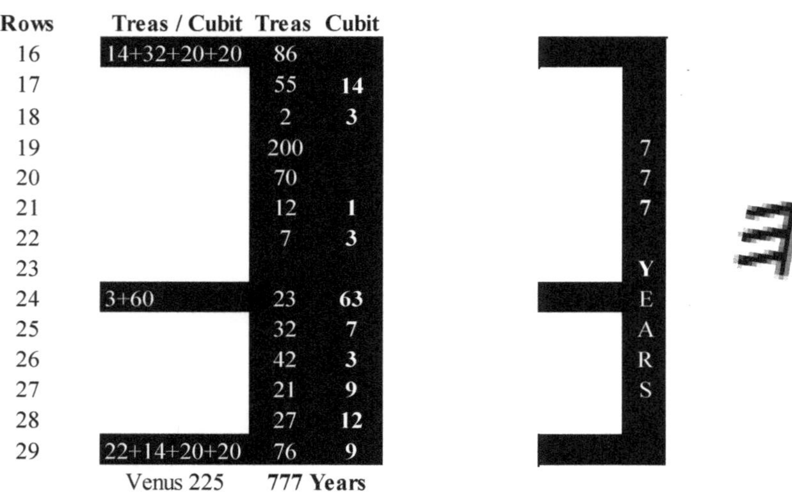

Rows	Treas / Cubit	Treas	Cubit
16	14+32+20+20	86	
17		55	14
18		2	3
19		200	
20		70	
21		12	1
22		7	3
23			
24	3+60	23	63
25		32	7
26		42	3
27		21	9
28		27	12
29	22+14+20+20	76	9
	Venus 225	777 Years	

The next paleo letter was also with *he* or H but it was formed from two parallel illustrations the first of which included the orbit of Venus and its long-cycle of 777 years as shown in Illustration 2. The orbit of Venus included the treasures in sequence from Row 33 down to the 4 treasures only on Row 39 while the 777 years included the cubits and treasures in sequence from Row 37 down to the 80 treasures on Row 49 but not the cubits on that row. There were two spurs one of which was on Row 39 and the other on Row 48 of the module. It was preordained to multiply the three numbers of 13, 7 and 4 on Row 39 to get 364, which compared to Enoch's 364 day solar calendar. Likewise, the numbers 2, 300 and 20 on Row 48 were multiplied to get 12,000 and that total compared to the Zoroastrian time of the long dominion of 12,000 years.

---

[9] Image from the public domain.

The second part of the display involved the second age of Seth at 807 years which was displayed in the checksums. With this module, there were three spurs which contained the extra treasures with the numbers 2, 4 and 20. Just like the numbers on Rows 39 and 48 were multiplied so were the three numbers 3, 60 and 2 to give 360 as shown in the illustration. Therefore, there were three outstretched arms, which made the illustration look like the Paleo-Hebrew letter *he*. The modular version with the combined illustrations is shown alongside the Paleo-Hebrew letter *he*, which is represented by H in the English language.

Illustration 2:

Venus and 777 Years   Seth with 807 Years   807 and 777 Years with Letter he

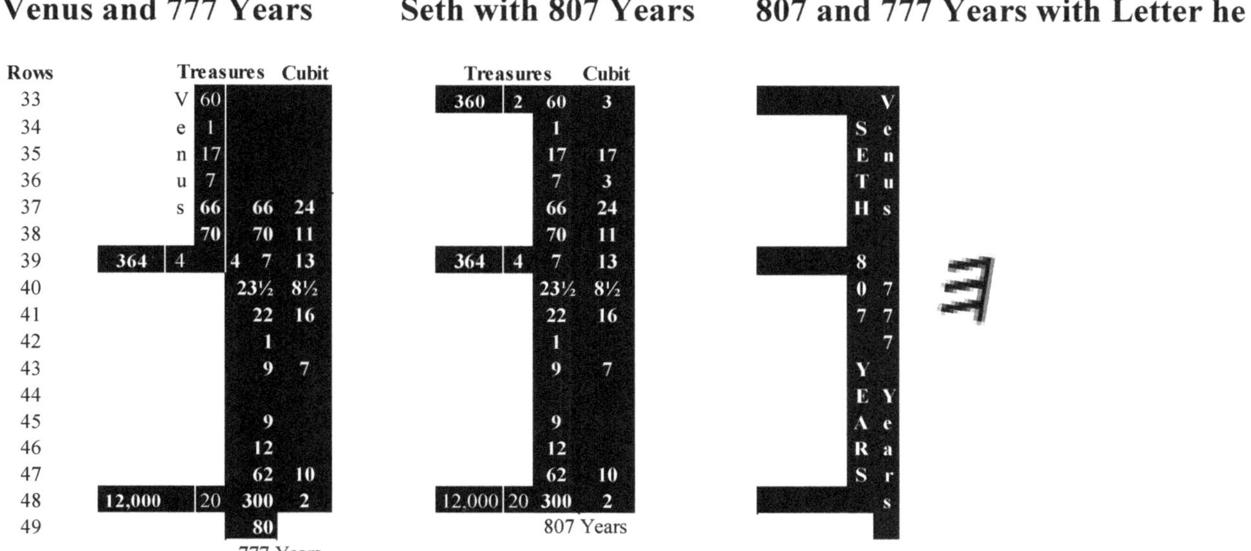

The second age of Seth at 807 years featured as an image of the Paleo-Hebrew letter *he* and that seemed strange because his age was one of the checksum totals. However, it would appear that the scribes of the copper scroll were making a statement with Seth for he had a background in astronomy. The first century historian Josephus had stated that Seth and his family were inventers of that peculiar sort of wisdom which concerned the heavenly bodies and their order. (Josephus p 32) To safeguard the celestial data from the oncoming flood, they wrote the contents on brick and also inscribed it on stone. It therefore seemed relative that on Row 35 on the copper scroll, there was a reference to an inscribed stone monument. The inclusion of Seth in displaying a Paleo-Hebrew letter suggests that the data on astronomy on the copper scroll originated back in pre-historic times.

The next configuration resembled the Paleo-Hebrew letter which is called *Wah* and known as W in the English language and it is shown in Illustration 3. It was formed from the orbit of Mars at 687 days on the right hand side with its long-term cycle of 79 years on the left hand side. In the centre was the long-term cycle of Saturn at 707 years. The modular version is shown alongside the Paleo-Hebrew letter Wah.

Illustration 3:

Mars and Saturn   Modular Display with Letter *wah*

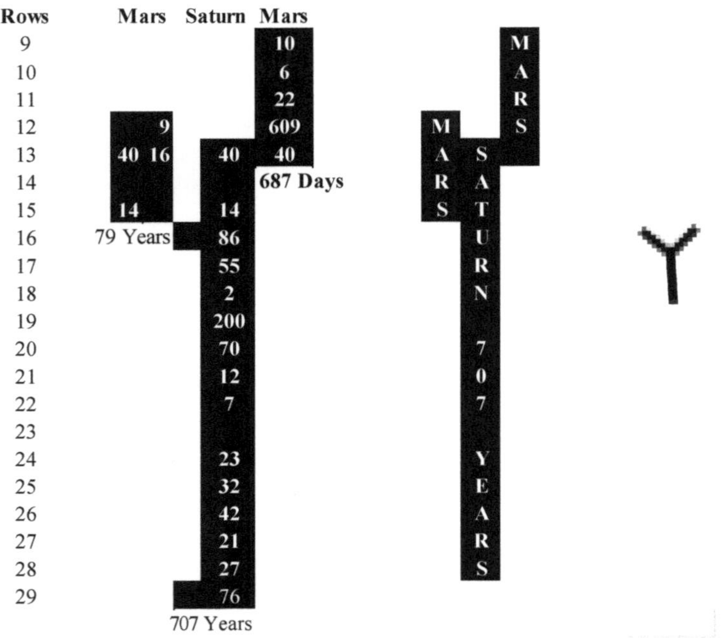

Rows	Mars	Saturn	Mars
9			10
10			6
11			22
12	9		609
13	40 16	40	40
14			687 Days
15	14	14	
16	79 Years	86	
17		55	
18		2	
19		200	
20		70	
21		12	
22		7	
23			
24		23	
25		32	
26		42	
27		21	
28		27	
29		76	

707 Years

There was a second configuration which also resembled the Paleo-Hebrew letter Wah or W and it was with three tables with totals of 777 as shown in Illustration 4. It modular display is shown alongside the Paleo-Hebrew letter Wah.

Illustration 4:

Three Displays of 777 Years   Modular Display with Letter *Wah*

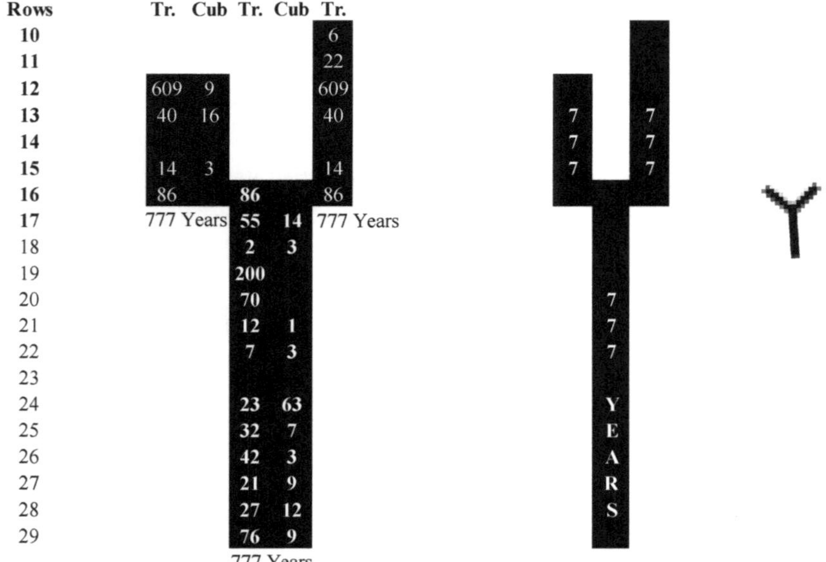

Rows	Tr.	Cub	Tr.	Cub	Tr.
10					6
11					22
12	609	9			609
13	40	16			40
14					
15	14	3			14
16	86		86		86
17	777 Years		55	14	777 Years
18			2	3	
19			200		
20			70		
21			12	1	
22			7	3	
23					
24			23	63	
25			32	7	
26			42	3	
27			21	9	
28			27	12	
29			76	9	

777 Years

The final configuration resembled the Paleo-Hebrew letter Yod or Y and it began with the 70 treasures on Row 38 and included the cubits and treasures in sequence down to the 5 treasures only on Row 58. The total at 1,653 as years was 777 days by 777 times with 16 intercalary days of an overlap. It had three spurs with extra treasures with 4 on Row 39, 20 on Row 48 and 5 on Row 58 as shown in Illustration 5. The numbers to form Enoch's 364 day solar calendar was in the first spur and it seemed preordained to enter 364 as days in the spur. Enoch's second age at 300 was in the second spur and by multiplying the three numbers in that row, the result at 12,000 compared to the Zoroastrian time of the long dominion of 12,000 years. The final spur involved only one number and so no multiplications were intended.

There was another configuration that ran in parallel with 1,653 years and it included the cuits and treasures in sequence from Row 40 to Row 57. The total at 1,554 or 777 + 777 compared to the long-term cycle of Jupiter at 1,554 years. There was just one spur and it was on Row 48 and its three numbers multiplied out to 12,000.

Illustration 5:

777 + 777 years - Jupiter   777 × 777 Days   Modular Display with Letter *Yod*

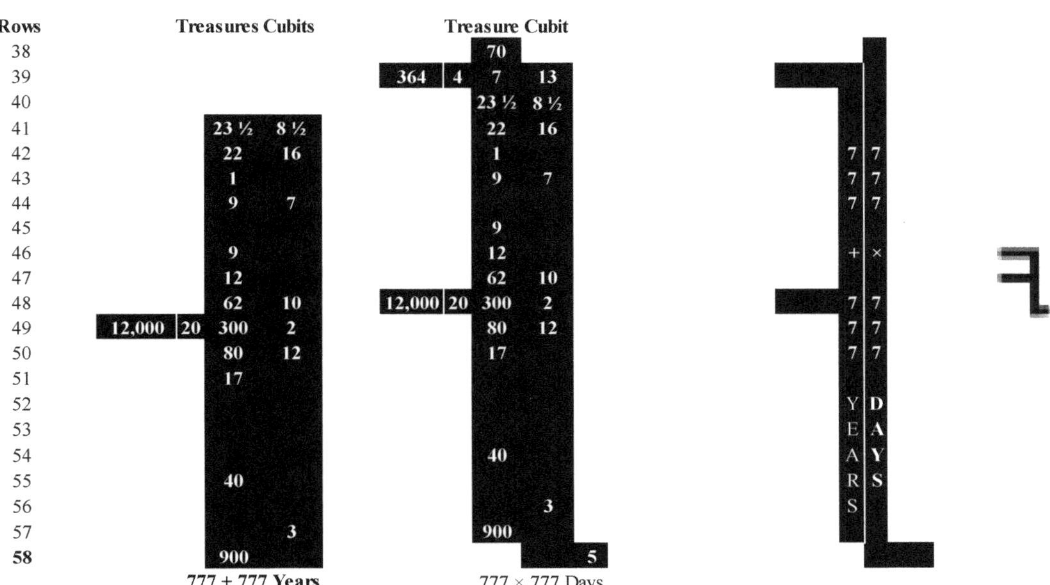

The modular version of those two configurations is shown alongside the Paleo-Hebrew letter Yod. It can be seen that a modular version of Illustration 777 × 777 would have been sufficient to form the Paleo-Hebrew letter Yod. However, there was a good reason for also including Jupiter with 777 + 777 in the modular version because the ancient astrological sign for Jupiter was the Paleo-Hebrew letter Yod.[10]

Summary

There were two separate configuration which resembled the Paleo Hebrew letter *he* with its English display of H. There were also two separate configurations which resembled the Paleo-

---

[10] Alexander Jones, *Astronomical papyri from Oxyrhynchus: (P. Oxy. 4133-4300a)*. (American Philosophical Society ISBN 978-0-87169-233-7. 1999).

Hebrew letter *Wah* with its English display of W. There was one configuration which resembled the Paleo-Hebrew letter *Yod* with its English display Y but it was complimented by a parallel configuration which included the long-term cycle of Jupiter at 777 + 777 years. Those duplicate displays showed that the scribes of the copper scroll ensured that there could be no ambiguity about the presence of those Paleo-Hebrew letters having been intended. The modular configurations which had the numbers 777 forming the Paleu-Hebrew letters are shown in Illustration 6. The illustrations were drawn within the rigid structure of a spreadsheet table but they need a graphic designer to apply the finishing touches. It is vital to display the configurations as they appear on the copper scroll because it shows they were positioned to clearly spell out the autograph of YHWH.

In agonising over the identity of the spelling with the letters, the translator Emile Puech had referred to Beth-Shem as unlikely to be the temple of Jerusalem for it would spelled as "*the temple of the name*" (= *YHWH*).[11] It was very close to the bone especially as the entries with Beth-Shem and 600 talents on the copper scroll were at the foot of the Y module to spell YHWH. It was a supreme indication of YHWH because the only listing of 600 talents in the Bible was with the weight of gold, which was used to decorate the holiest house in Solomon's temple, which was the house of YHWH.

---

[11] Emile Puech, 2015 p 109.

Illustration 6: The Divine Autograph of YHWH on the Copper Scroll

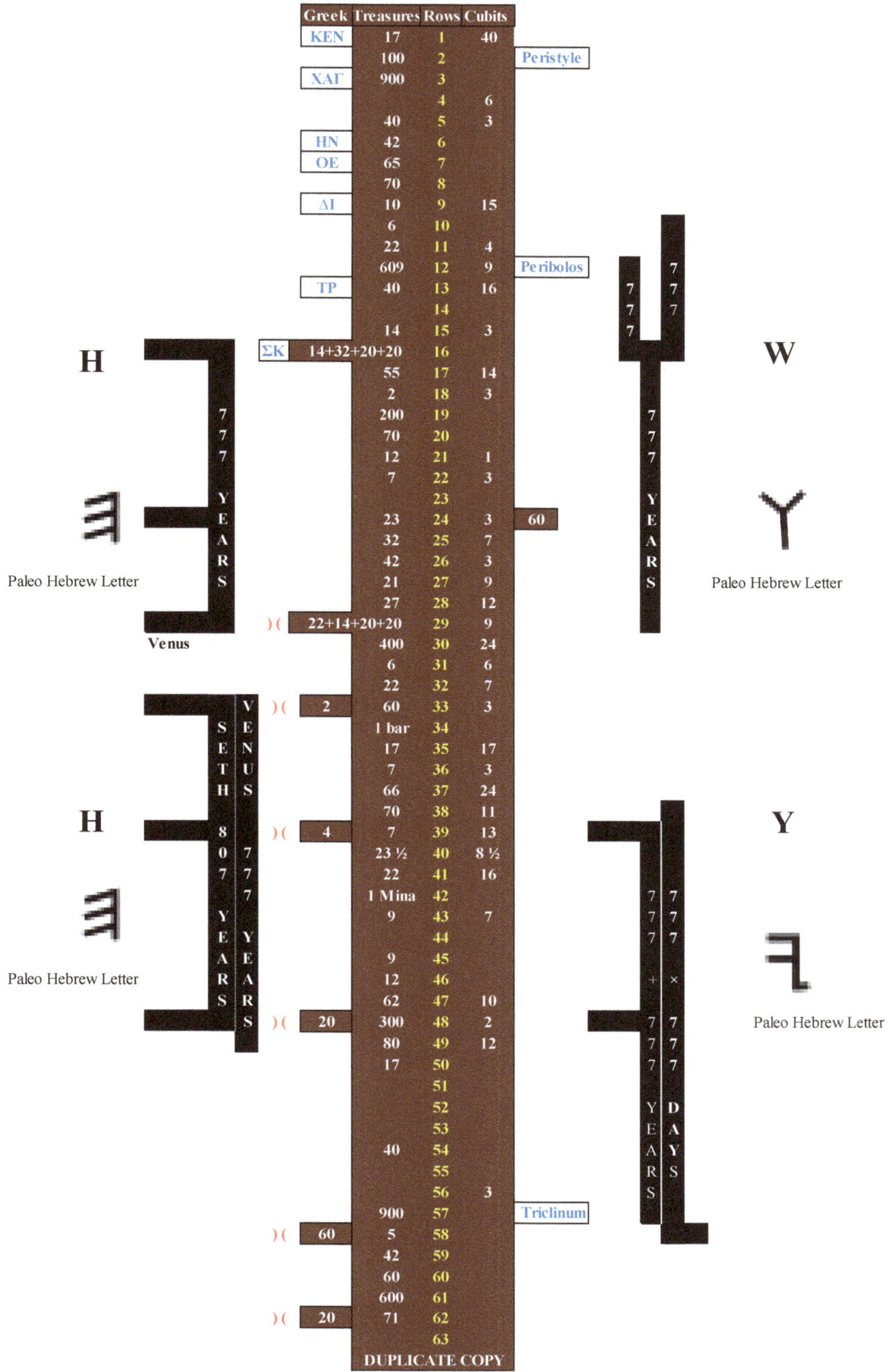

Part 2

The Duplicate Inventory

Chapter 7

Numbers Hidden in Plain Sight

In the course of the last two centuries, scholars have identified that the first five books of the Bible with the Torah, were re-edited over five hundred years before Jesus and huge amounts of extra text were inserted. From detailed studies of the etymology and syntax of the text, scholars have been able to identify the editorial work of at least five different writers.[12] Curiously, a major part of those insertions were hosts of numbers including practically the whole Book of Numbers. What made the revisionism so incredible was where those book keeping accounts with the numerical data were so bizarre such as with unbelievable old ages of people together with exaggerated population sizes. To make matters even more unusual, the numbers were set among stories of events that happened centuries beforehand.

Those insertions changed the whole complexion of the Bible and made it possibly the first fabricated account of historical revisionism. In that ancient world of superstition, anything out of the ordinary was attributed to angry gods such as with thunder and lightning. Therefore, it was perhaps not unusual to find that some of the biblical re-writers delved into fantasy where they wrote about whispering snakes, talking donkeys and miracles that were the stuff of fairy tales. There was one of the rewriters who had none of those distractions but instead he/she was obsessed with numbers. That writer even employed double entry methods to ensure that those numbers would retain their original values. For instance, the measurements of the tabernacle of Moses were listed twice in the Book of Exodus and that made it easy for copyists to validate the accuracy of the numbers.

The revised biblical epic included the exodus out of Egypt and it turned fiction into Hollywood reality for its spellbound audience. In effect, the biblical writers had successfully pulled the wool over the eyes of every generation for two and a half thousand years until modern research methods blew their cover. Opinion is divided among academics about this re-editing and some hold the traditional line that the Torah was written by Moses while others accept that the books were re-edited. Unfortunately, academics have concentrated on the reasons for the re-editing and have largely ignored the numerical insertions. The principal question to be asked was why did the re-editors insert reams of numbers? Why had the re-editors listed men living to be over 900 years old? For rational minded people, those ages were nonsensical and that was possibly why some numbers in the Bible were avoided like the plague by most academics.

The insertion of numbers in the Torah suggested that they must have been of tremendous importance to the biblical elite establishment and especially to the re-editor who has been named by scholars as the writer P. It was generally accepted that the inner circle of priests in most societies did not readily share important information with the uninitiated. However, if they wanted to safeguard the knowledge for posterity, how were they to achieve that aim? To preserve their sacred scrolls, the scribes hid them in caves by the Dead Sea and that included the copper scroll. Because the treasures on the copper scroll were a disguise to safeguard tables of astronomy, it was likely that the original data had been repackaged and encoded as an assembly kit of numbers in the Torah and other books of the Bible. And that is what the biblical writers did because it will be shown how many of the indices of the copper scroll calendar were also encrypted in the Old Testament.

---

[12] Richard Elliot Friedman, *Who Wrote the Bible?*

It must rate as one of the most successful camouflages in history. The associated methods of encryption with some of the numerical data were equally intriguing because the numbers were hidden in plain sight. So brilliant was the disguise, that the inherent configuration escaped the prying eyes of every generation over the centuries. It was a pious fraud that was done with imagination but at last the wonderful secret knowledge of the biblical writers can be revealed.

Chapter 8

Identifying the Duplicate Inventory

The last column of the copper scroll stated that there was a duplicate copy that listed the measurements and treasures item by item and it was hidden in a cave with tombs at its mouth. This duplicate copy was not found with the other Dead Sea scrolls nor was it found at any other location. But were the archaeologists looking in the wrong places for the duplicate inventory because there were amazing similarities between the data on the copper scroll and the data in the Old Testament. For instance, there was a reference to a cave on column seven of the copper scroll where there was a listing of 400 talents. In comparison, it outlined in the Book of Genesis how Abraham had paid 400 shekels of silver to purchase a cave in order to bury his wife, Sarah. (Genesis 23:16) A cave and 400 talents on the copper scroll compared to a cave with 400 shekels in the Bible. The comparison between the details on the copper scroll and the Old Testament was again evident where in column four it outlined as follows:

"Between the two boulders in the valley of Achor, right at the midpoint between them, dig down three cubits: two cauldrons full of silver coins. In the red dry well on the edge of the Wadi Atsla: silver coins totalling two hundred talents. In the dry well on the north east of Kohlit: silver coins totalling seventy talents. In the cairn of the Secacah Valley, dig down one cubit: twelve talents of silver coins." (Wise)

In the same column were the valley of Achor, 200 hundred talents of silver and a cairn. The cairn was listed by another translator as a memorial mound of stones. The signposts from the scroll with the number 200 led to the Book of Joshua where a descendant of the tribe of Judah called Achan stole 200 hundred shekels of silver. (Joshua 7:21) Achan hid the treasure beneath his tent but the Lord was angry at such a wicked deed and punished the Israelites in battle. Joshua sought out the guilty party and identified Achan as the culprit. He had him stoned to death and the Israelites heaped up a large pile of rocks upon his body. It stated in the Book of Joshua that the place was called the valley of Achor to this day.

Contrast the similarity between the copper scroll and the incident with Joshua. The same numerical figures of silver were evident with 200 talents in the scroll as compared to 200 shekels in the Book of Joshua. Both texts identified the location as the valley of Achor and both had a memorial mound one being of stones as compared to rocks over Achan. Achan was from the tribe of Judah whereas the column of the copper scroll ended by referring to the valley of Sekaka, which happened to be apportioned to the tribe of Judah. Finally, Achan had hidden the treasure and the scroll referred to hidden treasure.

The comparisons continued where it was noticeable that some of the numbers on the copper scroll without the cubits or the treasure weights were also in the Old Testament. For instance, the first two numbers on the scroll were 40 and 17. In comparison, it outlined in the Book of Genesis that the flood started on the 17th day and it rained for 40 days and nights. Another pair of numbers was also obvious where there were the numbers of 70 talents and 10 talents on the scroll. These two numbers compared to the biblical weights of 70 shekels and 10 shekels in Chapter 7 of the Book of Numbers. It was not a chance sighting with just single numbers but instead, the two matches were with two couplets involving the numbers 40 and 17 and 70 and 10 in both sources.

The observations with matching couplets on the copper scroll and in the Old Testament led to the employment of a biblical search engine to seek out more matches. It was a fruitful exercise because the searches led to many locations with gold and/or silver treasures in the Old Testament. The difference was that the treasures were listed as talents on the copper scroll whereas their counterparts in the Old Testament were with shekels. The matching process was also employed with some words on the copper scroll such as with *'round mouth'* as outlined earlier relative to Pi and a circle. It was noticed that the word *'dovecot'* was cited three times on the scroll and it had been identified by translators as a bird house with many openings. Bird houses are normally associated with pigeon lofts. By association, the paranormal instinctive ability of homing pigeons was not too unlike the matching process where the prime location had to be literally landed on. If this was intended by the scribes of the copper scroll, then it was a clever cognitive use of symbolism to convey an intended activity such as homing in on the numerical targets.

There were four pairs of numbers at the beginning of the copper scroll, which had been arranged as couplets where they were bordered in between sets of Greek letters. It was those couplets that led to checking for matches of them in the Old Testament. Using couplets would enhance the matching process for it would be as rare as finding twins. The Top Ten locations of where the pigeons came home to roost with the couplet matching process are now outlined.

<u>Match 1</u>

The first match was with the pair of numbers of **40** and **17** together on <u>row one</u> of the copper scroll. It led to the Book of Genesis where it outlined that the flood began on the **17**th day of the second month and it rained for **40** days and nights. To reinforce the notion of couplets it specifically emphasised how Noah had brought the animals on board the ark *'two by two.'* The scene with Noah and the flood involved a, encrypted demonstration of the 777 day calendar and this will be outlined in detail in a forthcoming chapter.

<u>Match 2</u>

The next important match led to a scene, which had a haunting similarity with the search for items of treasures. On <u>row thirty three</u> of the copper scroll there were instructions to dig **3** cubits and find **60** talents. This couplet led to Chapter 6 of the Book of Ezra where Darius ordered a search for a **roll** in the house of rolls where the plundered treasures from Solomon's temple were stored in Babylon. A **roll** was found and therein there was a record which outlined how Cyrus the king had previously made a decree that the house of God in Jerusalem was to be rebuilt and its dimensions were to be **60** cubits high by **60** cubits in breadth. The details went on to say that the house was finished on the **3**rd day of the month of Adar.

Therefore, there were the two numbers of **60** and **3** on the scroll and **60** and third (meaning 3) in the Book of Ezra. It had outlined in the **roll** by Cyrus that the **golden** and **silver** vessels, which had been carried off from Jerusalem, were to be returned to the temple. The search by Darius for a roll in the house of rolls was not too unlike what this matching exercise was trying to do. After all, the original Old Testament would have been a series of papyrus rolls at the time the original coy of the copper scroll was written as was attested to by the Dead Sea scrolls documents themselves.

<u>Match 3</u>

The matching process with couplets continued where it stated on <u>row nine</u> of the copper scroll to dig down **15** cubits to find **10** talents. The trail led to a couplet in the Book of Leviticus where it outlined in the chapter how the women over 60 years of age were valued at **10** shekels of silver and the men were valued at **15** shekels of silver. (Leviticus 27:7) It was a couplet with **10** and **15** together and it was like a helpful prompt where the men and women were been converted in value to silver shekels. The biblical writers had obviously not heard about gender equality in those bygone days. The matching exercise continued and encountered two more couplets of numbers with **60** cubits and **3** cubits on <u>row twenty four</u> together with **60** talents and **5** gold talents on <u>row fifty nine</u> of the scroll. These couplets were found in the same verses in the Book of Leviticus thus resulting in a total of three successful matches relative to humans being valued as silver shekels.

Match 4

The pointing to treasures in the Old Testament continued where it stated on <u>row twenty seven</u> of the copper scroll to dig **9** cubits to find **21** talents. The matching process led to Chapter 52 of the Book of Jeremiah where it told about Zedekiah who began to reign as king when he was **21** years old. In his **9**th year the Babylonians besieged Jerusalem and burned Solomon's temple before taking away all of the treasures to Babylon. Just like the lists of treasures on the copper scroll, the treasures that were plundered from Solomon's temple were also listed in that same chapter of the Book of Jeremiah. The list included pillars of brass, the brazen sea, caldrons, shovels, snuffers, bowls, spoons, basons, firepans, candlesticks, cups *"and that which was of gold in gold, and that which was of silver in silver, took the captain of the guard away."* (Jeremiah 52:17-23) Therefore, the couplet of **21** and **9**th in Jeremiah was another clear pointer to treasures where it told about the gold, silver, brass and bronze treasures of Solomon's temple. It was peculiar how the quote stated about *"gold in gold"* and *"silver in silver"* for it was like a suggestion of a '*match for match*' exercise with gold and silver as pertained in this comparison exercise.

Match 5

On Row 5 and 6 of the copper scroll there were the numbers 40 and 42 and they matched up with the 42 stops the Israelites made on their 40 years in the desert wilderness. The 42 stops were listed singularly and had to be counted to get the total. On Row 21, there were the numbers 1 and 12 and they compared to the one tribe of the Levites and the twelve tribes of Israel. The two censuses of the tribes of Israel will feature in one of the chapters.

Match 6

The next hit on target was with **70** silver talents and **10** talents as a couplet on <u>rows eight and nine</u> of the scroll and it matched with **70** shekels of silver and **10** shekels of gold in Chapter 7 of the Book of Numbers. It was a direct hit with silver and gold and it was part of a trend, which had talents from the scroll but had shekels in the Bible. It said on the copper scroll that the duplicate inventory would list the treasures item by item. With this latest hit, the copper scroll couplet had led to the biggest set of tithe offerings in the Old Testament where each of the leaders of the twelve tribes gave three silver and gold offerings. All of the items were listed together with their weights in shekels of silver or gold. Each tribe donated one silver charger weighing 130 shekels, one silver bowl weighing 70 shekels and one golden spoon weighing 10 shekels. There were twelve such listing with silver and gold. The target with those tithe offerings was enhanced where there was a sum total of all of the gold and silver offerings at the end of chapter in the Book of Numbers. Those totals had the numbers 24, 60, 60 and 60 and all four matched up with the same four numbers dispersed on the copper scroll.

Match 7

A match with **2** cubits and **20** vessels on <u>row forty eight</u> of the copper scroll led to those two numbers together in chapter eight of the Book of Ezra where it stated as follows: *"twenty basons of gold, of a thousand drams; and two vessels of fine copper, precious as gold."* (Ezra 8:27) There were **20** basons of gold and **2** vessels of fine copper. It was the only listing of the word copper in the KJV of the Old Testament and it stated that it was as precious as gold. It was noticeable how the earlier quote about a roll of records from the search by Darius had outlined how the treasures from Jerusalem were referred to on that roll or scroll. It seemed opportunely suggestive where Ezra had referred to *"two vessels of copper"* and the copper scroll was actually found in two separate parts in the cave at Qumran. Ezra may have been the redactor who conducted the final re-editing of the Torah and shaped the theme of the other books in the Old Testament. (Friedman p 218)

Match 8

There were four number with 55, 2, 200 and 70 on Rows 17 to 20 on the copper scroll and they led to the era of King Hezekiah and his son Manasseh, his grandson Amon and his great grandson Josiah. King Hezekiah made a burnt offering, which consisted of **70** bullocks, **100** rams and **200** lambs. Two of those numbers with **70** and **200** matched up with the two numbers together on the scroll. (II Chronicles 29:32) The numbers **55** and **2** were together on the scroll and remarkably, those two numbers matched up with the reign of King Manasseh and his son Amon. Manasseh reigned for **55** years and Amon reigned for **2** years. (II Kings 21:1, 19)

Those two numbers were at the hub of the 777 day calendar to map out the period of 117 years. It took 55 times the interval of 777 days to reach 117 years and there were a fraction less than 2 days of an overlap. When the ages that the four kings reigned were added together, the total came to 117 years. Therefore, three of the indices with the 777 day calendar yardstick were all stashed together in the era of Hezekiah to his great grandson Josiah with 117, 55 and 2 and there were also the two numbers of 70 and 200 with a burnt offering. Hezekiah made a second burnt offering and its numbers revealed why the Torah and other books of the Old Testament had been covertly re-edited around the era of the king. It was to insert the indices of the copper scroll calendar as the collective numbers of animals in sacrificial burnt offerings. The indelible ink of blood from those animals would last the test of time, in what must rate as the most profound form of numerical encryption ever devised especially as the numbers were hidden in plain sight. How the calendar indices were encrypted as the numbers of animals in the burnt offerings with be outlined in a chapter of this book.

Match 9

The existence of a duplicate inventory was listed in the last column of the copper scroll and it stated that the document would outline the measurements and the treasures item by item. In the same column on the scroll, it outlined about the vessels of silver and gold whose total was 600 talents. When the weight of 600 talents was entered onto the search engine there was only one appearance and that was where Solomon was building the temple. (II Chronicles 3) It outlined that the most holy house in the temple was 20 cubits long and 20 cubits wide and it was overlaid with 600 talents of fine gold. It was truly divine where there was the numbers 600 and also 20 together in the most holy house in Solomon's temple and those two numbers were also together at the end of the scroll where the duplicate inventory was referred too. For it to be in the holiest of holiest sanctuaries within Solomon's temple was a spell binding encounter, which made the appeal of terrestrial treasure sites fade into insignificance.

There was a second hit with the 600 gold and silver pieces that was equally divine. The challenge was to search to see how many times those two words with *gold* and *silver* appeared in the Old Testament. It would have been a daunting task for investigators to conduct because it would have required them to read all of the books in the Old Testament. But now the task was simple with the use of a search engine. The word *gold* and the word *silver* were entered onto the search engine where the KJV of the Old Testament was applied. There were 336 listings of the word *gold* and 264 listing of the word *silver*. Their combined total came to 600 listings of the two words. It was a perfect match with 600 on the scroll and 600 listings of the words *gold* and *silver* in the KJV of the Old Testament. This part of the quest had first led to the 600 talents of gold in the most holy house within Solomon's temple and now there was a match made in heaven with the total of words gold and silver in the most sacred set of books, which became the Old Testament.

<u>Match 10</u>

The next match led to cubits in the Bible and it arose from the very last number on the copper scroll. This final numerical listing pointed to a location where **20** minas were hidden. It was therefore a surprizing bonus to find that the last listing of the number **20** in the Old Testament related to a flying scroll and it was in the Book of Zechariah. The text read as follows: *"Then I looked up and saw a flying scroll! And the angel asked me, "What do you see?" I answered him, "I'm looking at a flying scroll. It's 20 cubits long and 10 cubits wide."* (Zechariah 5:1, 2) From the copper scroll to a flying scroll seemed intended and so those measurements of **20** cubits and **10** cubits became the new couplet for the matching exercise. It led to the porch in King Solomon's temple which was 20 cubits long and 10 cubits wide. (I Kings 6:3) Being led into the porch was a wonderful invitation to enter into the temple from the scribes in antiquity especially as the matching process had earlier led to the holy of holiest chamber.

There was also another couplet with the two numbers of **2** silver bars and **200** silver talents on <u>column four</u> of the copper scroll, which led to Solomon's temple. This couplet matched up with **2** pillars on which **200** pomegranates were carved. (I Kings 7) The last column of the copper scroll had stated that the duplicate inventory would list the measurements and all the items, item by item. The two separate couplets together with the 600 talents were dead on target because there was a list of the number of cubit measurements to build Solomon's palace and temple in the chapter.

The total of the cubits that were given in Chapter 7 of the first Book of Kings to build the palace and the temple was **386.5** cubits. In comparison, the total of the cubits on the copper scroll was 383.5 cubits with Puech, 382.5 cubits with Wise and those totals were almost an exact match with the 386.5 cubits in the Old Testament chapter. However, Lefkovits had listed a further 3 cubits on <u>row fifty seven</u> of the scroll and that number had been validated as original by the checksums. It meant that those 3 cubits could be added to the total of 383.5 cubits by Puech bringing the grand total to **386.5** cubits. This made it a perfect match between the copper scroll and Chapter 7 of the first Book of Kings with the total of 386.5 cubits.

Those Top 10 hits were just the initial examples of what had been revealed by the matching process. They had led to treasures of gold and/or silver in the Bible together with a roll and a scroll and much more. That the matching employed couplets of numbers made the targets all the more precious. Added to this was the match with the large single number of 600 talents of gold and silver on the copper scroll, which matched with the 600 listings of the words *gold* and *silver* in the King James Version of the Old Testament. There were three matches, which led to the building of King Solomon's temple and palace. It was with those building projects where a jackpot of cubits was encountered with a total at 386.5 cubits. (I Kings Chapter 7) This number was an exact match with the 386.5 cubits listed on the copper scroll.

The results from the matching process will come as a shock to those people who believe that there was nothing hidden in the Bible and that it was an open book without covert codes or secret formulas. Yet in the Books of Daniel and Revelation, there were very distinctive references to a scroll or book within a book on which great secrets were written. And now the evidence was emerging to show that the copper scroll held the secret to unlock what was written in the book within a book in the Bible.

Chapter 9

The Dimensions of the Copper Scroll

There were several references to a secret scroll or book in the Bible and the associated text indicated that nobody could read what was written on the document as it was sealed. (Rev. 5:1-9, Rev. 10:2-10, Isaiah 29:11, Daniel 12:4 and Ezekiel 2:9-10) Now that the mysterious calendar and tables of astronomy have been deciphered, it was possible that the secret scroll was the original document that the data on the copper scroll was copied from. It was outlined earlier that the last number on the copper scroll with 20 minas led to the last appearance of the number 20 in the Old Testament. This was in the Book of Zechariah where there was a <u>flying scroll</u> whose dimensions were given as 20 cubits long and 10 cubits high. It was an enormous size for a scroll because it would have been as big as the front wall of a single storey house. This flying scroll led to checking the dimensions of the copper scroll.

Wolters had outlined that the copper scroll was made out of three sheets and each were roughly 30 centimetres by 80 centimetres in size. There was confusion over the length of a biblical cubit where it was given as 21 inches in the appendix with the book by Josephus or as 18 inches with several Internet sources. It was felt that the length with 21 inches from the appendix in Josephus was the safer option to use. The 30 centimetres converted to 0.56 cubits and the 80 centimetres to 1.494 cubits. This would have made the length of the scroll 1.494 by three = 4.5 cubits long approximately though allowance would have to be taken for possible overlapping when the sheets were joined together. For the purpose of this exercise, it is taken for the moment that the size of the copper scroll was 0.56 cubits wide and 4.5 cubits long.

The length of the scroll in Zechariah at 20 cubits long and 10 high was certainly not a match. Because the copper scroll had led to those two dimensions with the number of 20 minas it was possible that the 20 cubits and 10 cubits in Zechariah were intended as a couplet to springboard the search a step further and look for a similar matching couplet elsewhere in the Old Testament. The two numbers of 20 cubits and 10 cubits were therefore entered into the search engine and it stopped at chapter six of the first Book of Kings and chapter four of the second Book of Chronicles where Solomon was building his palace and the temple. It was a perfect match where it was also with 20 cubits and 10 cubits as the size of the porch in the temple. The flying scroll had led us in to the porch of the temple and it seemed to be an invitation to look inside the building to see if there was any evidence that would link the secret scroll with the copper scroll.

Solomon was portrayed as the wisest man in the Old Testament and several couplets of numbers had led to his palace and temple where the match with the total of the cubits on the copper scroll at 386.5 cubits was found. The pointing of the finger to Solomon continued where in <u>column five</u> of the scroll, the translation read as follows:

"At the head of the Aqueduct...Secacah, on the north, under the big stone, dig three cubits: seven talents of silver. In the crevice which is in Secacah, on the east of Solomon's reservoir: vessels of tribute. And their document is beside them. Above Solomon's canal, towards the big stoning heap, sixty cubits, dig three cubits, twenty three talents of silver. (Wolters p 41)

The scroll had referred to Solomon's reservoir and in order to home in on it, the word <u>reservoir</u> was entered into the search engine. The search engine stopped at chapter seven of the first Book of Kings where it stated:

"Hiram also made a sea of cast metal ten cubits from brim to brim, circular in shape and five cubits and 30 cubits in its inner circumference. Under the brim, completely encircling it, were two rows of gourds inlaid as part of the original casting, ten to a cubit. The sea stood on top of twelve oxen. Three faced north, three faced west, three faced south, and three faced east. The sea was set on top of them, and their hind parts faced the center. <u>The reservoir</u>, which held about 2,000 baths, stood about a handbreadth thick, and its rim looked like the brim of a cup or of a lily blossom. Hiram] also made ten bronze water carts. Each one was four cubits wide, four cubits long, and three cubits high." (I Kings 7:23-27 International Standard Version)

The comparison between the scroll and the Old Testament location was better than what any terrestrial map could outline. Just like the copper scroll, the quote from scripture referred to <u>Solomon</u>, <u>reservoir</u>, <u>north</u>, <u>east</u>, <u>60 cubits</u> and <u>3 cubits</u> and it led to <u>Solomon's temple</u>, which was <u>60 cubits</u> long. There were three oxen facing <u>north</u> and <u>east</u> and a <u>reservoir</u> of baths together with <u>3 cubits</u>. It was a septuplet match with words and numbers in Verses 23 to 27 of Chapter 7 of the first Book of Kings. But there was a touch of imperfection in the quote above from the Bible where it had made reference to a circle and it implied that the numerical value of pi was **3**, which was way off the mark of 3.14. Sometimes such blunders by the scribes were deliberate attention seeking prompts. Therefore, it was time to see if anything lay behind such a blunder by the architects who designed Solomon's temple.

Because of the large amount of listings of cubits in the chapter, the attention was to see if the dimensions of the copper scroll were detectable in Solomon's temple. The dimensions of the copper scroll at 0.56 cubits wide and 4.5 cubits long could not have been presented in biblical times because there was no such thing as decimals in those days. There were however fractions such as ¼, ⅓, ½, ⅔ and ¾. The nearest 0.56 cubits could be presented by the scribes was therefore ½ a cubit and with 4.5 cubits it was 4 ½ cubits. The next step was to see if there was any sign of those two numbers in the chapter with Solomon's temple.

There was one listing of ½ a cubit in chapter seven verse thirty five as follows: *"And in the top of the base was there a round compass of half a cubit high."* That catered for the ½ cubit. Then the attention turned to look for the 4 ½ cubits. In verse thirty one of chapter seven it stated as follows: *"And the mouth of it within the chapiter and above was a cubit: but the mouth thereof was round after the work of the base, a cubit and an half:* This was a decoding exercise and the cryptic presentation in the verse could be expected. It would have been a giveaway if the scribes had presented the 4 ½ cubits in the shop window and so it was expected to find a cryptic exhibition to make the number less detectable.

The statement referred to *a mouth that was round and 1 ½ cubits.* This was supposed to be describing the base but it could not be because it was square in shape with dimensions of 4 cubits by 4 cubits. It stated that the borders were four square and not round. There appeared to be two separate *objects* in the picture and one of them was both round and foursquare. A scroll is round but when it is opened it is rectangular. Taking the one measurement of 1 ½ cubits as the diameter of the *circular object* and using the ratio of 3 for the implied value of pi with respect to the molten sea, the result with 1 ½ cubits by 3 was 4 ½ cubits. It was a perfect match with 4 ½ cubits for the circumference of the *object* as compared to 4 ½ cubits in length for the copper scroll. If this object was a cylinder it would open up to be rectangular and be 4 ½ cubits long.

There were some confusing details in the description of that object but there was a second appearance of that measurement in the same verses of the chapter with respect to the wheels of the chariots. The diameter of each chariot wheel was 1 ½ cubits high and thus its circumference in biblical terms was 4 ½ cubits as compared to 4 ½ cubits for the length of the scroll.

There was still one more throw of the dice and it followed in the footsteps of the 1 ½ cubits multiplication that was hidden behind the computation involving pi. This was where there was the possibility that the scribes may have encased the dimensions of the copper scroll in a checksum total. The two dimensions of the scroll were 0.56 and 4.5 cubits. Thus, the checksum total was 5.06 cubits. The biblical search engine showed that there were twenty five listings of *5 cubits* in the Old Testament and one of them would have to stand out in the crowd to be identified as special. Sure enough, one listing of 5 cubits was found in the verse where the value of pi was defined as follows: "*And he made a molten sea, ten cubits from the one brim to the other: it was round all about, and his height was five cubits: and a line of thirty cubits did compass it round about.*" (I King 7:23) The measurement of 5 cubits as the height of the molten sea was in the middle of the two measurements, which identified the value of the biblical pi. And the length of the copper scroll had been found in the computation with Pi relative to the base beneath the molten sea. It was another indication that the measurements of ½ a cubit wide and 4 ½ cubits long with the copper scroll had been copied from chapter seven of the first Book of Kings.

Solomon's temple proved to be the epicentre of the treasure trail and the matches was a testament of this position where the length of the copper scroll at 4 ½ cubits was unveiled from beneath the erroneous value of pi in the base of the brazen sea while the breadth of ½ a cubit was found as the diameter of the round compass on top of the base. Then the checksum total of 5 cubits was found within the listing of the pi formula as the height of the brazen sea.

Chapter 10

The Time of the Long Dominion of 12,000 Years

The matching process with couplets of numbers had originally started with the first two numbers on the copper scroll where the instruction was to go 40 cubits to find 17 talents. These two numbers were a couplet because they were immediately followed by a Greek letter **KEN.** The two numbers identified with Noah and the timing of the flood as set out in the Book of Genesis. It stated that the flood began on the 17th day of the second month and it rained for 40 days and 40 nights. (Genesis Chapter 7) To reinforce the location with the target there were the optimal number with 2nd followed by 3 cubits and 40 silver talents on the scroll and these matched up with the 2nd month and the 40 nights in the flood story together with the reference to the 3 wives of Noah's sons. In just two sentences in Genesis there were those five numbers with 17th, 2nd, 40, 40 and 3 and those five numbers were all in column one of the copper scroll. It was a quintuplet and that was a match in lotto jackpot figures.

The next two numbers on the scroll were 100 gold ingots and 900 talents as a pair because they were fenced in between the two sets of Greek letters **KEN** and **XAΓ.** There was however no matching pair together with 100 and 900 in the Old Testament. But this was a decoding process and every piece of information had to be treated as a possible part of the building blocks. In this regard, there was the number 100 with Noah's son Shem who was 100 years old when he became a father. There was a listing of a <u>sepulchre</u> with the 100 ingots and in contrast, Shem's name and ages were like engravings on a tombstone in the Book of Genesis.

There was the listing of <u>immersion pool</u> and <u>reservoir</u> in <u>column one</u> of the scroll and those words identified with water, which in turn identified with the <u>flood</u>. There was the number 600 in <u>column twelve</u> on the copper scroll and it appeared alongside <u>springs</u> and the name Beth-<u>Shem</u>. In comparison, Noah was 600 years old when the <u>springs</u> of the deep burst open to cause the flood and of course his sons name was <u>Shem</u>. There was also the listing of 300 talents on <u>column ten</u> of the scroll and it was to be found in the vicinity of a <u>pond</u> or <u>pool</u> of water. In comparison, the ark was 300 cubits long while the <u>pond</u> or <u>pool</u> of water linked up with the scene when the flood was abating. Therefore, the flood story in Genesis seemed to be a target from the copper scroll.

The reason why the copper scroll had pointed to the flood story will now be outlined. It is an exercise in numerical wizardry and mental logic that a gifted prodigy had created to show future generations how the ark had sailed forward in solar time but back in time in accord with sidereal time. The scribe had used a dating system with the journey of the ark and it conformed to the 777 day method for measuring time.

The first sign that there was sometime amiss in the flood story was with an anomaly with the ages of Noah and his son Shem. It stated in the Book of Genesis that Noah was five hundred years old when he became the father of triplets, one of whom was Shem. It also outlined that the flood finished on the end of Noah's 600th year. However, later in the story it stated that Noah's son Shem became a father when he was 100 years old, which was listed as two years after the flood. That was fake news for Shem would have been 102 years old when it was two years after the flood. It appeared that the scribes had tempted us with an intellectual challenge where the episode of the flood contained possibly the first numerical riddle in written existence.

The next anomaly came to notice when tracing the dating events in the saga of the flood as outlined in the Book of Genesis. Read the three chapters in order to get a greater appreciation of the timing details. The relevant times given for the events at the beginning of the flood are listed below and to make the presentation more user-friendly, the names of the months that we use today are utilised. It should be stated that ancient numbers and arithmetic were very different than what we used today. The timing details were as follows:

All went into the Ark on the 17th day of the 2nd month and the rain started: **17th February**

It rained for 40 days and 40 nights and the waters rose for 150 days
until the ark was 15 cubits above the mountains. This would date the
event forward to 17th day of 7th month: **17th July**

But it then stated that the ark rested on Mount Ararat on the
17th day of 7th month: **17th July**

There was a major problem for how could the ark rest on Mount Ararat on the 17th day of the 7th month when the waters were 15 cubits above the mountains on the same day and had not the time to recede? The ark had come up against a barrier worse than an iceberg and it was amazing to find that this blunder had never featured prominently in previous biblical commentary. It was back to the drawing board to investigate what the story tellers had in mind when they devised the puzzling dating system in the flood saga.

Time on Earth Different than Time at Sea

Biblical academics have established that there were two versions of the flood story standing back to back. One of those versions was in the earthly realm where it simply rained for forty days and forty nights. But the other version was in the cosmic realms where it stated that the windows of the heavens were thrown open and the fountains of the deep were broken open. Because the ark sailed up to the heavens and with such a precise dating schedule, cognises has to be taken of solar and sidereal time. The difference between the solar year and the sidereal year was outlined earlier but for convenience, the details are outlined again as follows:

- Our calendar is based on the solar year, which is measured against a fixed point on the landscape such as a sun dial and it is 365.242 days long.

- The sidereal year is measured against a fixed star in the heavens and it is 365.256 days long.

The sidereal year is therefore longer than the solar year by a little over twenty minutes. It was already shown that the biblical astronomers seemingly made theoretical projections where the tiny time period of twenty minutes added up to one day in 72 years and fourteen days in 1,000 years. It gave a meaning to the phrase in the second Book of Peter where *"with the Lord a day was like a thousand years."* In the epic saga of the flood, the scribes also used time on land to represent solar time and time at sea to represent sidereal time.

By measuring time with the 777 day method, it required 157 days to be added on to synchronise the calendar with 3,000 solar years and 197 intercalary days to be added on in 3,000 sidereal years. Armed with the knowledge of the 777 day calendar and its indices it was quite obvious that the leap days for solar time were on display in the flood story. The saga outlined that the rain started on the 17th day of the 2nd month and the waters rose for a period of 150 days. After that the waters receded for another 150 days. There were also two periods with Noah waiting for 7 days plus 7 days when he sent out the dove which returned the second time with an olive leaf in its beak. These collective periods added up to two distinct intervals with 157 days plus 157 intercalary days. The two intervals fitted like gloves for they equated exactly to the leap days, which had to be added on to synchronize the 777 day calendar when projected out over 3,000 plus 3,000 solar years.

The period of 197 days to represent 3,000 sidereal years was not openly discernible in the flood saga. But while drawing up a chart to show the complete dating of the flood epic from beginning to the end, a very unusual picture emerged. The mental arithmetic suggested that the timing details of the flood epic also dated back in time to the tune of sidereal time. This seemed surreal until the complete timing details of going forward in time and going back in time were mapped out as shown in Illustration 7.

Illustration 7: The Blue and Yellow Routes of the Ark through Solar and Sidereal Time

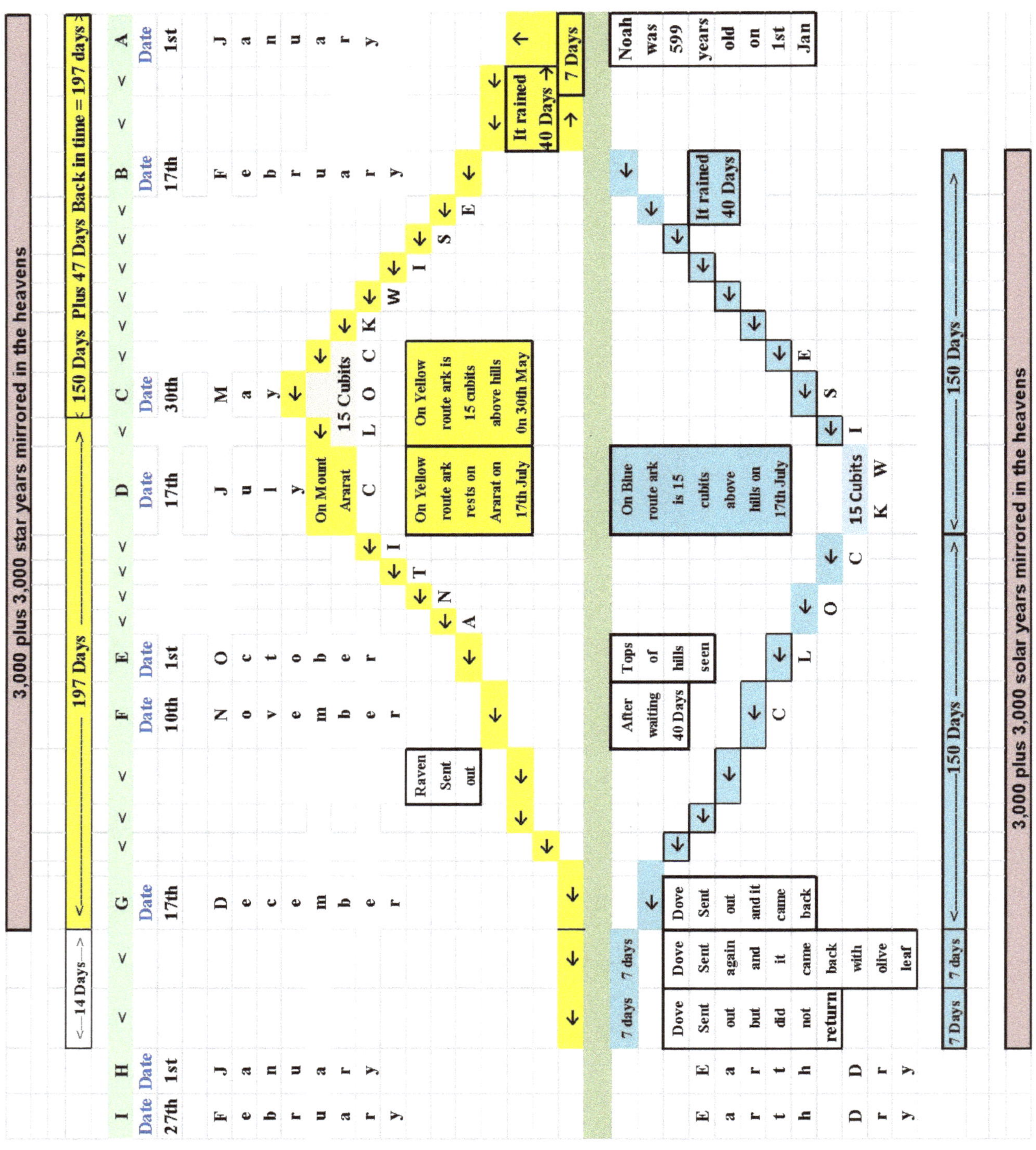

In was an amazing spectacle where this illustration formed naturally into the shape of a huge ship with sails. The details may seem overwhelming to digest but approach the diagram as you would with using a street map to find your way around a foreign city. In simple terms the route the ark took forward in accord with solar time is outlined in blue. The events began on February 17th and follow the arrows and you will see that there were two periods of 150 days plus two periods of 7 days to when the flood ended on the last day of December of that same year. Thus, there were two combined periods of 157 leap days on the blue route to mirror two periods of 3,000 solar years when measured with the 777 day formula. That was the journey on the blue route and it was in accord with solar time.

The sidereal time route was paradoxically, back in time as shown on the yellow route. The starting day was the same on the yellow route where it began on February 17th when the rain began. Follow the arrows back in time with the 40 days and nights rain together with a 7 day waiting period, as was outlined in the Book of Genesis. That brought the dating schedule back to the 1st January. Then continue back in time through the previous year starting with January, February, March and April until an extra 150 days had elapsed and that was on the 30th May. In all it was a total of 40 + 7 + 150 = 197 days, which equated to the same period in intercalary days for 3,000 sidereal years. On that date of the 30th May on the yellow route the ark would have been fifteen cubits above the mountains.

Tracing the path back in time from the 30th May to the 17th of July the waters would have had 47 days to recede. That was the date in the timing schedule where it stated that the ark rested on Mount Ararat on the 17th day of the 7th month. The problem of the ark resting on Mount Ararat was resolved for the waters had those 47 days to recede on the sidereal route back in time. Continuing back in time from the 17th July for another 150 days it brought the schedule to the 17th day of December. That made it an extra period of 197 days with 47 +150 days. Therefore, there were two periods of 197 days back in time from when the flood began on the 17th February to the 17th December of the previous year. These equated to two periods of 197 intercalary days with sidereal time when projected out over 3,000 plus 3,000 sidereal years.

This puzzle has to be studied like the moves on a chest board so it may help to retrace the two routes again as follows:

- On the blue route follow the arrows forward in time from the 17th February and note the timing in the blue boxes. You will see where the 150 days plus 150 days plus 7 days plus 7 days are listed for the complete period to the last day in December. Therefore, there were two combined periods of 157 days plus 157 days on the blue route and they were in accord with solar time. The 40 days and nights of rain ran in parallel with the 150 days that the waters rose.

- On the yellow route trace the arrows initially back in time starting on the 17th February and it took in the 40 days and nights rain plus 7 days that Noah waited. Then the route switched on the 1st January back in time through the previous year. Follow the arrows and note the dates in the yellow boxes. The days added up to 47 days plus 150 days (197 days) to when the ark was fifteen cubits above the waves on the 30th of May. The schedule showed the ark traveling back anticlockwise in time on the yellow route and the 40 days and night ran in series with the 150 days. Follow the yellow route back in time to the 17th day in July (seventh month) when the ark rested on Mount Ararat. The anomaly was solved for the waters had 47 days to recede to let the ark dock on the mountain. Continue on the yellow route back in time for another 150 days making it a total of 47 + 150 = 197 days to end on the 17th December of the previous year.

It was the '*double speak*' of two separate routes which confused the issue with the ark resting on Mount Ararat on the 17th July (seventh month) on the yellow route whereas it would have been fifteen cubits above the mountains on that date on the blue route.

The Period of 777 Days

There was still one more surprise in store where it seemed so odd how two different dates were listed of when the flood ended. The schedule stated that the earth was dry on the 1st day of January of the following year. Then the scheduled repeated that the earth was dry and it appeared that it was on the 27th February of the same years. There was a very good reason for having those 57 extra superfluous days built into the story from the 1st January to the 27th February when the earth was dry. The biblical year with the flood comprised of twelve months of thirty days each thus giving a total of 360 days. Therefore, it is necessary to trace the two different journeys of the ark. From the 17th day of February to the end of the Noah's 600th year, there were 313 days. Going back in time from the 17th day of February, there was 47 days in Noah's 600th year and 347 days through Noah's 599th year until the 17th December. But the Ark did not stop there because it continued until the 27th day of February (2nd month) and this was verified with the statement about Shem becoming a father two years after the flood. It was two years after the flood ended on the sidereal route back in time. Therefore, the total number of day were as follows:

$$313 + 47 + 347 + 13 + 57 = 777$$

The designers had written in the main indices of the calendar formula with 777 days into the timing details and that was the purpose of the 57 extra days to the 27th February of the following year.

Zoroastrianism

What mortal eye could look upon such a majestic display that the scribes had prepared for the dual journey of the ark and not be captivated by its splendid numerical logic? Who were those visionaries who could project time into the future and demonstrate in a thought provoking matrix, the difference between solar and sidereal time over the period of 12,000 years? They were possibly five centuries before Hipparchus because it is reckoned that the flood saga was rewritten between 722 and 609 BCE. (Friedman p 210)

The period of 12,000 years forged a link to the Zoroastrian time of the long dominion of 12,000 years. Zoroaster was a Persian prophet whose teachings were of a dualistic battle between good and evil. There was a good God named Zurvan who sacrificed for 1,000 years that he might have a son. Two sons were born, and one was named Ohrmazd who was good, and the other was Ahriman who was evil. Those two gods were in conflict in a duel which would continue over four finite periods of 3,000 years of material creation on earth. At the end of the long dominion of 12,000 years, good would prevail, Ohrmazd would triumph over Ahriman and finite time would merge with infinite time.

Those three periods of 1,000 years, 3,000 years and 12,000 years were all detected on the copper scroll. The period of 12,000 years had identified with the time of the long dominion and in that regard Whitrow outlined the beliefs of the heretical form of Zoroastrianism as follows:

"A distinction was made between Zurvan akarna (infinite time) and 'Time of the Long Dominion' (finite time), the later lasting 12,000 years (the number twelve being associated with the twelve signs of the Zodiac) is the period of struggle between good and evil. In fact, the whole raison d'etre of finite time appears to have been to bring about that conflict of good and evil which leads to the ultimate triumph of the good." (Whitrow, P 16)

The philosophy of good and evil was at the heart of Judaic and Christian belief and featured in some of the other Dead Sea scrolls as an apocalyptic battle between the sons of light and the sons of darkness. (4Q491 – 4Q497)

The display with the four periods of 3,000 years in the flood story confirmed that the purpose of the Reed 777 day calendar was with the religious philosophy which lay behind finite time with the Zoroastrian period of the long dominion of 12,000 years. As outlined by Whitrow, the raison d'etre of finite time verses infinite time was to go through the stages of conflict between good and evil, which would lead to the ultimate triumph of the good. It can therefore be gleaned that the moral of the flood story was with the theme of good and evil. On earth the journey was in solar time and the evil mortals on the ground perished in accord with God's command. In contrast, the journey back in time was in accord with sidereal time of the heavens and all the good people with Noah and his family on board the ark survived to tell the tale.

All through the centuries the Jewish and Christian ministries had been preaching in a vacuum unaware of the divine like cosmic knowledge of the biblical writers and the majestic qualities of the 777 day calendar that mastered time itself.

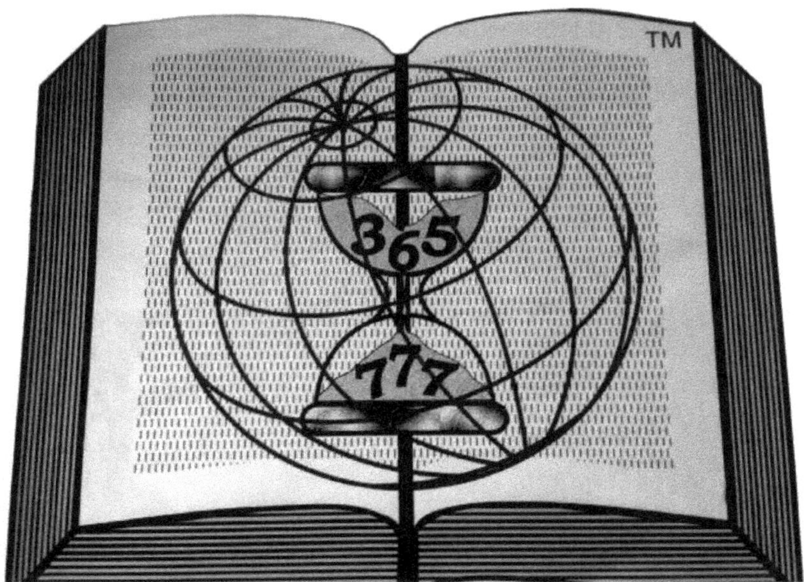

The two numbers with 365 and 777 were the duplicate keys to unlock the numerical encryption in the Bible.

Chapter 11

The Unique Method of Biblical Encryption

There was only one number between the Greek letters of HN and OE and it was with 65 gold ingots. The number 65 compared with the first age of Enoch and also with his grandfather Mahalaleel, which were listed in Chapter 5 of the Book of Genesis. It seemed as if the writers had inversed the couplet arrangement from the copper scroll to the Bible with having those two listings together of the number 65? The next number on the copper scroll was 70 and it set up another couplet match where there were 65 and 70 on the copper scroll and those figures compared with 65 for the first age of Mahalaleel and 70 for the first age of his father Cainan. Therefore, there was that extra definite pointer with 65 and 70 in sequence as a couplet to substantiate that Enoch and Mahalaleel were the target of the matching exercise.

The two ages with 65 years added up 130 years and it was noticeable that this was the first age of Adam. To find out if the number 130 with Adam was a new figure in the matching process, it was entered into the search engine and it led to twelve listings of that number in Chapter 7 of the Book of Numbers. This encounter was where each of the leaders of the tribes of Israel offered one silver charger weighing 130 shekels of silver in the most diverse set of tithe offerings in the Old Testament.

The next couplet on the scroll was with 70 silver talents and 10 talents and they were paired in between the Greek letters of OE and ΔI. The couplet also led to the same chapter in the Book of Numbers as had happened with the number 130. Following on from the offering with a charger weighing 130 shekels of silver, there was one silver bowl weighting 70 shekels and one spoon weighing 10 shekels of gold in tithe offerings. It was a direct match with silver and gold treasures though the listings on the scroll were in talents whereas the listings in the Bible were in shekels. There were now the three numbers with 130, 70 and 10 together in the matching process. The couplet with 70 and 10 had been a direct hit on target whereas the number 130 had travelled on a circular route like a boomerang to finally hit the target.

There was an extra pointer to the tithe offerings where there were 24 cubits on <u>row thirty</u> of the scroll and its matching number was with 24 bullocks in the sum up of the numbers in the peace offering, which was at the end of chapter seven of the Book of Numbers. There were also 60 rams, 60 goats and 60 lambs in the same sum up in the chapter. In comparison, there were four listings of the number 60 on the scroll with 60 cubits, 60 talents, 60 talents and 60 talents. It meant that there were the numbers 24 cubits, 60 cubits, 60 talents, 60 talents and 60 talents set apart on the scroll but there were in sequence as 24 bullocks, 60 rams, 60 goats and 60 lambs in the Book of Numbers.

The four numbers were not together on the copper scroll but they were linked by descriptions relating to water. It began with the number 24 cubits on <u>row thirty</u> was with the word <u>reservoir</u> and then with 60 cubits on <u>row twenty four</u> which was at a <u>canal.</u> The 60 talents on <u>row thirty three</u> was with the word <u>well spring</u> or <u>water outlet</u> while the number 60 talents on <u>row fifty nine</u> was followed by the word <u>fountain</u>. Therefore, the four numbers of 24, 60, 60 and 60 were all linked by water on the scroll. These spurious words that were listed to describe the sites such as with reservoir were obviously the coded means of linking numbers together, which were set apart on the scroll. It was therefore a match with a quadruplet set of numbers, which certainly confirmed that the tithe offerings in the Bible were a priority on the agenda with the scribes of the copper scroll. They reason why they were targeted will now be outlined.

To understand the encryption in those tithe offerings, it was necessary to take account of how the biblical writers counted. In biblical times, counting was in a series of ones and there was evidence in the Bible to show that that the Hebrews counted in that manner. There were two examples of counting in ones the first of which was in Chapter 7 of the Book of Numbers, which the copper scroll had led to. In that chapter, it outlined that the leaders of the twelve tribes of Israel made many different tithe offerings over the period of twelve days. There was a proliferation of the number 'one' in those offerings with one charger, one bowl, one spoon, one bullock, one ram, one lamb and one goat. There was also a similar series with the optimal numbers beginning with the 1st day and continuing with the animals which were to be of the 1st year without blemish. It was very relevant that the counting in a series of ones began with the offering on the 1st day for it indicated that there may be a time related function in the counting method. Out of curiosity, the number of ones and the optimal number 1st in the twelve days of offerings were added up and the total came to 111. Today we write that total as 111 but in ancient times it would have been one hundred and eleven separate ones.

The second example of counting in a series of ones was in the Book of Joshua where all the dead kings were counted with the king of Ai, <u>one</u>, the king of Jericho <u>one</u>, the king of Jerusalem <u>one</u> etc. all the way up to 31 dead kings. (Joshua 12:9-24) To check if there was a connection between the two listings of counting in ones, a simulation exercise was carried out on a calculator of counting in lots of 111 days. The outcome was surprising because after counting out 102 lots of 111 days, the count reached 31 solar years to the very day. That was the breakthrough and the result was sufficient to show that those two exercises in counting in ones were linked. It indicated that the writers of the Bible had covertly left the evidence of how to count the days in lots of one hundred and eleven days and the 31 dead kings symbolised 31 solar years.

Counting the days in series of ones up to one hundred and eleven days was possibly conducted on an abacus because it would have been the perfect instrument to serve that purpose. After counting out six lots of 111 days, the count would have reached 666 days. After seventeen counts in that higher format of 666 days, it would have reached 31 years to the very day.

In my research work several years previously, I had entered all the numbers in the twelve days of offerings in Chapter 7 of the Book of Numbers onto a spreadsheet. That was what made the difference for I became aware of a strange feature, which materialized before my eyes. Each of the twelve tribes made a burnt offering of one bullock, one ram and one lamb. In the tabular format the numbers appeared as follows:

In that tabular format and without the animals, the figures became visible as the merged number 111. It seemed to be an optical illusion until I counted up the number of ones and optimal numbers of 1st in the tithe offerings and the total came to 111.

There was another surprise in store and it had to do with the Sabbath of seven years. Allegro had interpreted the name *Kohlit* on the copper scroll as *"all of the tithe and stored seventh year produce"*[13] In the same column Puech had interpreted *"the total of the tithe and the treasure of the*

---

[13] John Allegro Column 1, Item 4.

Sabbatical year." The Sabbath year was every seven years. The translation by Martinez of this section referred to *"the second tithe made unclean."* In the Damascus document of the Dead Sea Scrolls it referred to things which were hidden including his holy Sabbath. The quotation was as follows:

"He instituted his covenant with Israel forever, revealing to them things hidden, in which all Israel had gone wrong: His holy Sabbath, His glorious festivals, His righteous laws, His reliable ways... He opened up to them." (Damascus Document 3:13-16)

The quote was very explicit relative to a covenant with Israel, revealing to them hidden things including the holy Sabbath. The leaders of the twelve tribes of Israel made those tithe offerings to the Lord before Moses. In the Dead Sea Temple scroll 11Q19-20 it stated *"She must not touch your pure things for seven years, nor eat peace offerings until seven years have passed."* There seemed to be something special about peace offerings and seven years.

The reference to hidden things and the Sabbath of seven years bore fruit when the numbers of animals in the peace offering were entered onto a spreadsheet. There were **two** oxen, **five** rams, **five** goats and **five** lambs. In the textual presentation, the numbers looked like **two, five, five, five**. However, in the tabular format on the spreadsheet a new bigger number became visible as follows:

In that tabular format the merged number of 2,555 was evident. If that mirage with the merged number of 2,555 held true then it was a covert way to present seven years because 365 day by seven was 2,555 days. It was the same period of seventh year that Allegro had translated and also with Puech who had interpreted the text as the Sabbatical year. The words on the Damascus document now made sense about the holy Sabbath being hidden but revealed to Israel. It was through the tithe offerings, which were made by the tribes of Israel where the merged number 2,555 was revealed from where it lay hidden in plain sight. (It should be noted that the original numbers would have been presented in Hebrew letters and not in the numerals of 1, 2, 3, 4, 5, 6, 7, 8, 9 and 10, which we use today for they were Arabic in origin and were only developed long after the Bible was written)

When you have grasped the ingenuity of the encryption encoding method, the relationship between the two merged numbers of 111 and 2,555 can be explained. The calendar scroll found at Qumran had surprised biblical scholars for even priestly rosters were attuned to solar time. Now here in the peace and burnt offerings was the key formula for measuring seven solar years. Simply put it meant counting out the days one by one up to 111 days and repeating the exercise 23 times and the total came to 2,553 days. This was just two intercalary days short of seven years. This methodology would have been very simple to administer on an abacus.

It is necessary to point out the mathematical side effects of those new merged numbers. In the example with the number 111 the lambs represented units, the rams tens and the bullocks hundreds. But in the example with the number 2,555 the lambs represented units, the goats tens, rams hundreds and the oxen thousands. It showed that the bullocks, rams and lambs were a form of notation, which would be on par with our terms of €, $, Ω and ф or other type notations. Indeed, the British unit of weight, which has caused many a blush on weighing scales, is a natural term for it is called '*stones.*'

Because of finding the merged number of 111 in the tithe offerings, an examination was carried out of the numbers from the copper scroll for evidence of that number. It transpired that the totals of the numerical listings themselves added up in the vicinity of 111. To make sure that this was the correct result, six translations of the copper scroll were checked and the results were as follows:

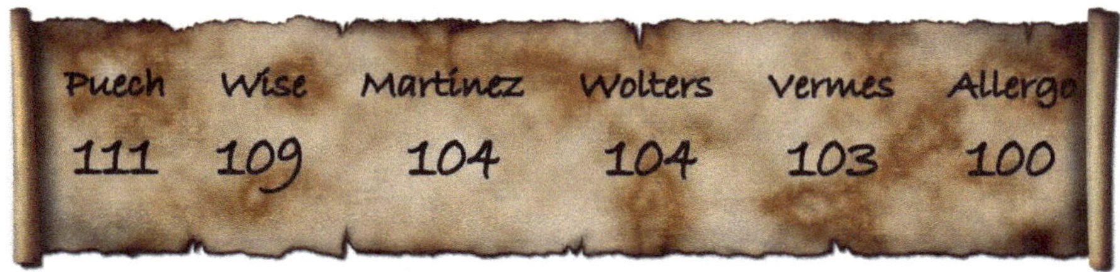

It would appear that counting in a series of ones up to 111 was on the minds of the copper scroll writers because Puech had listed 111 items.

From the practical standpoint the exercise in the tithe offerings was a basic demonstration on how to count in ones. The result in our contemporary way of counting was 111 but in biblical times it would likely have been one hundred and eleven ones in a row on an abacus. However, the merged number of 111 from the burnt offerings indicated that the biblical mathematicians had developed the same method as our contemporary way of presenting one hundred and eleven ones as 111. Can you just imagine the tribal leaders as they made those tithe offerings? One charger, one bowl, one spoon, one bullock, one ram, one lamb and one goat were the tally. It would be a suitable exercise for school children rhyming off the basic units of counting.

There was one other piece of the jigsaw to be revealed. A search was conducted among all the books which make up the Old Testament for the name Jacob and his pseudonym Israel. The total listings in the Revised KJV for the two names were as follows:

The total came to 2,555, which was also the number of days in the Sabbath of seven years. It is important to point out that the result applies only to the words Jacob, Jacob's, Israel and Israel's. The position with Jacob working a period of seven years or 2,555 days for the right to marry Rachel was obviously a prompt of those 2,555 listings of his names in the Old Testament. It was also the second example (witness) to illustrate that the findings with the numbers of 600 listings of the words gold and silver were intended. The copper scroll had opened up a highway through the Old Testament to give us a completely new insight into how the associated books were written and compiled.

Chapter 12

The Reed-777 day Calendar in the Bible

The copper scroll had revealed that the indices of the 777 day formula were one of its main treasures. Therefore, the matching process will resume and show how the scribes had pointed to where those same indices of the 777 day formula were located in the Old Testament. The exercise began with the couplet of **15** cubits and **10** talents on <u>row nine</u> of the scroll and it led to King Hezekiah where he lay dying. The king did not want to die and so the prophet Isaiah produced a miracle when he turned back the clock of Ahaz by **10** degrees and this resulted with the king living another **15** years. The scroll was vibrant with clues in fingering Hezekiah because there were two associated words in the vicinity of those two numbers of 10 and 15 and they referred to a *'burial chamber and gates.'* When Hezekiah was sick he wrote *"I shall go to the gates of the grave."* (Isaiah 38:10) There was a *'burial chamber'* on the scroll and a *'grave'* in scripture and the word *'gates'* on both documents.

The matching process resumed and this time it involved four numbers, which were all together on the scroll from <u>column seventeen</u> to <u>column twenty</u>. These included a possible couplet with **55** silver talents and **2** silver bars and this pair of numbers was immediately followed by another possible couplet of numbers with **200** silver talents and **70** silver talents.

The matching process with those four numbers led to the era of King Hezekiah and his son Manasseh, his grandson Amon and his great grandson Josiah. King Hezekiah had already been fingered above but he again was pointed out by the scroll scribes where he made a burnt offering, which comprised of **70** bullocks, **100** rams and **200** lambs. Two of those numbers with **70** and **200** matched up with the two numbers together on the scroll. (II Chronicles 29:32) It was the second couplet, which had led to King Hezekiah and so it firmly identified with the king.

The numbers **55** and **2** were together on the scroll and remarkably, these two numbers matched up with the reign of King Manasseh and his son Amon. Manasseh reigned for **55** years and Amon reigned for **2** years. (II Kings 21:1, 19) Finally, the number 23 was on <u>column twenty four</u> of the scroll and it led to a statement by the prophet Jeremiah. The statement referred to *"from the thirteenth year of Josiah, the son of Amon king of Judah, even unto this day, that is the three and twentieth year."* (Jeremiah 25:3) Jeremiah had pointed the finger at Josiah and his **23**rd year, which seemed to be the possible target of the copper scroll.

The four kings with Hezekiah, Manasseh, Amon and Josiah had been fingered by the numbers from the scroll and two of the numbers had equated to the periods that two of the kings reigned. Furthermore, the numbers with **55** years and **2** years with the reigns of Manasseh and Amon were two of the numbers with the 777 day formula. (I.e., When 777 days are counted out **55** times it adds up to 117 years with an overlap of **2** leap days.) When the four periods that all four kings reigned were added up the result was as follows:

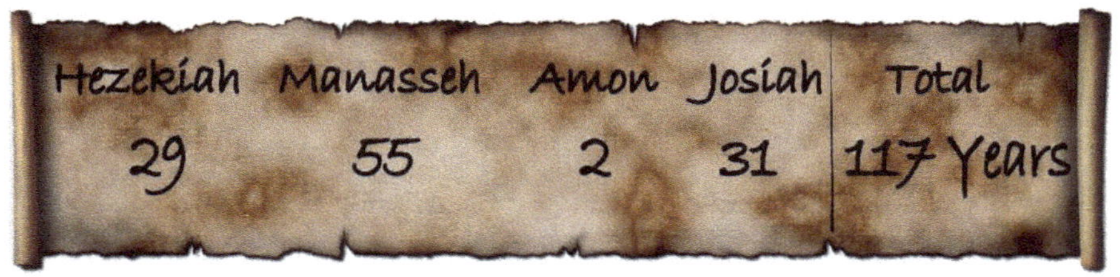

The total came to 117 years, which was one of the periods of the Reed 777 day formula.

The four numbers together on the copper scroll had led to the combined period of 117 years in the Old Testament. Two of those numbers with 70 and 200 had also to a burnt offering with 70 bullocks, 100 rams and 200 lambs, which was made by King Hezekiah. But the king also made another burnt offering and it comprised of **seven** bullocks, **seven** rams and **seven lambs**. (II Chronicles 29:2.1) On the spreadsheet the merged number of 777 could be visualized as follows:

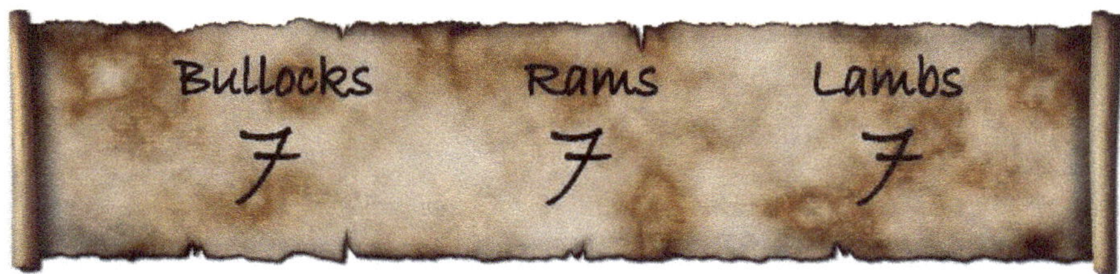

This merged number with 777 was the central number of the Reed 777-day formula and it too was hidden in plain sight.

King Hezekiah must have been at the heart of the re-editing intrigue because he was assigned the duty of displaying the 777 day formula for measuring time. Indeed, all four of the numbers of the 777 day formula with 777, 55, 2 and 117 had featured with the four kings thus pointing to that era as possibly when the re-editing had taken place. I decided to see how many listing of the word Hezekiah (s) were in the Old Testament and found that there were 117 such listings. It was the third example where words relating to important numbers were listed to give the totals of those numbers such as with 600 gold and silver listings and 2,555 listings for the names with Jacob and Israel.

The matching process continued and it was with a triplet of numbers with the numbers of **10** cubits, **2** cubits and **12** cubits together on the scroll. This triplet led to Chapter 29 of the Book of Numbers where a series of burnt offerings were made. There were three sets of those burnt offerings, which had the same numbers of animals with **one** bullock, **one** ram and **seven** lambs and these were offered for sacrifice. When one of those three burnt offerings was entered onto a spreadsheet the merged number of 117 became apparent as follows:

The merged number of 117 was one of the principal numbers of the Reed 777-day formula. Again, the merged number was hidden in plain sight but none could see.

In Chapter 28 of the Book of Numbers three burnt offerings were made of **two** bullocks, **one** ram and **seven** lambs. When the details were entered onto a spreadsheet the merged number of 217 appeared as follows:

The numbers 217 was another number from the Reed 777-day formula and it too was also hidden in plain sight.

The Periods of 100, 1,000 and 3,000 Years

We have already seen how the couplet with 200 and 70 on <u>rows nineteen</u> and <u>twenty</u> on the scroll had pinpointed a burnt offering, which was made by King Hezekiah where **70** bullocks, **100** rams and **200** lambs were sacrificed. Therefore, the number 100 to represent 100 years was located in that burnt offering. There were other burnt offerings to follow in the matching process where there was a reference on the copper scroll, which related to a priestly family at the time of Ezra. It was another lead for it led to two burnt offerings, which were made in the Book of Ezra. The first of these offerings comprised of **100** bullocks, **200** rams and **400** lambs. (Ezra 6:17) The numbers in those last two burnt offerings needed to be analysed.

The numbers began with the number 70 in the burnt offering, which was made by King Hezekiah and that number did not pertain to this particular part of the quest. However, all the other numbers in the two burnt offerings with 100, 200, 100, 200 and 400 did apply where their combined total was 1,000. Therefore, the numbers 100 and 1,000 had been located from just two sets of burnt offerings in the Old Testament.

The leap days for **1,000** solar years were **52** days. When both numbers were entered into the search engine it stopped in the Book of Nehemiah. It outlined that the patriarch had built the city wall and it was **1,000** cubits long and the wall was completed in **52** days. The search was for **1,000** and 52 together and both were in the Book of Nehemiah. It was also the only listing of **52** days in the Old Testament. (Nehemiah 3:13, 6:15) It is necessary to outline that while searching for the number of **1,000** it also led to King Solomon who made a burnt offering of **1,000** bullocks, **1,000** rams and **1,000** lambs when he was crowned king. (I Chronicles 29:21) There was the number **1,000** and of course the three numbers added up to **3,000** thus fulfilling the quest for those two numbers. Therefore, three more numbers of the 777 day formula with **100, 1,000** and **3,000** together with the **52** day period, had all been unveiled from the Old Testament.

The Millwheel of the Heavens

At the listing of the **3ʳᵈ** in column one, Puech and Lefkovits had a listed a <u>circular wall</u> while Wise had listed a <u>sealing ring</u>. Later in the scroll, Puech had listed a spiral staircase. Therefore, the prompt of a circle or circular motion was evident on the copper scroll. The number in that row in column one was **900** and it had been previously added to **100** to get the number of **1,000**. This total was added **3** times as prompted by the **3ʳᵈ** to get the number of **3,000**. I checked both those numbers of **1,000** and **3,000** on the search engine and both of them led me to Samson where he killed **1,000** men with the jawbone of an ass and also killed **3,000** people when he pulled down the temple of Dagon. In the adjoining row on the scroll there was the optimal number of **2ⁿᵈ**. Vermes had listed the word <u>colonnade</u> at site three and in comparison the number **2** led to the **2** <u>pillars</u> of the temple, which Samson pulled down and killed those **3,000** Philistines. There were the numbers of **2** pillars and **3,000** people together in the scene with Samson. (Judges 16:27-29) Leading up to that scene it had Samson turning the mill wheel round and round grinding the corn.

Samson had colossal strength but he lost it when Delilah deceived him. She inveigled him into revealing that his strength came from his seven locks of hair. She deviously told Samson's enemies the cause of his great strength and cut off his locks while he was asleep. The Philistines were therefore able to capture Samson and they blinded him thus making him unable to defend himself. However, while at the millwheel, his seven locks of hair grew again and gradually his unbelievable strength was renewed. When his colossal strength was restored, Samson pushed against the two main pillars, which held up the temple and the building came crashing down. A total of 3,000 people were killed in the escapade including the mighty Samson. The scene with Samson *turning the millwheel* was a mirror image of *the motion with the constellations of the heavens*. Samson's seven locks of hair saw the number 7 repeated over and over again as he pushed the millwheel round and round in a circle to ultimately form into the number 777.

There was another surprize hit in store where was the number of **6** cubits and the optimal number of **2ⁿᵈ** on <u>row four</u> of the scroll. When those two numbers were entered into the search engine it stopped at the walls of Jericho. Puech and Lefkovits had listed a <u>circular wall</u> and the scene at Jericho fitted the bill where it epitomised the circular motion where it stated: *"And the second day they compassed the city once, and returned into the camp: so, they did six days."*(Joshua 6:14) The number **6** and the word **second** had homed in on the first scene in the Bible where those two numbers were listed together. That scene was where there were **7** priests marching around the walls of Jericho **7** times over the course of **7** days. It was the ultimate display of the sevens, which adorn many parts of the Bible.

The Zodiac

Having displayed the images of the circular motion of the heavens the matching process will continue and unveil the constellations of the zodiac. It was noticeable that the number **60** was on <u>row fifty nine </u>of the scroll and there was another number **60** on <u>row sixty one</u> with the number **42** in between them. Thus, it seemed like a mini sequence so I added the three numbers together and the total came to **162**. This number of **162** compared to the first age of Jared who became a father to Enoch when he was **162** years old. It stated in the column that the treasure was hidden in a mausoleum while the names and ages of Enoch and his father Jared were like inscriptions on tombstones. Jared had been fingered by the scroll and when his first two ages were multiplied the result was $800 \times 162 = 129{,}600$. It was five times the length of the zodiac at **129,600** years.

We have seen earlier how the copper scroll had led us to King Hezekiah who was on his death bed. However, the prophet Isaiah intervened and turned back the clock of Ahaz by 10 degrees so that the king could live a further 15 years. The notion of turning back the clock was like breaking a time barrier for effectively, King Hezekiah rose from the dead. The sun dial of Ahaz was not an ordinary clock for if 10 degrees represented 15 years then the full 360 degrees of the clock would amount to 540 years. Hezekiah had to wait three days before the miracle took effect, which suggested four periods altogether of 540 years. I.e., 540 years when the clock was turned back and then three more periods of 540 years relative to waiting for three days. Therefore, the four steps would be 540 years, 1,080 years, 1,620 years and 2,160 years. The period of **2,160** years was recognizable as one constellation of the Zodiac.

It was shown earlier that the number 12,960 was unveiled from two couplets of numbers on the scroll. The scroll had also pinpointed Jared and his first two ages had multiplied out to five cycles of the zodiac at 129,600 years. Then the last computation with the clock of Ahaz unveiled one constellation of the zodiac. Therefore, the way was well prepared with those three examples relating to the zodiac for what was to follow. The search engine led to the Book of Ezra with the two numbers of **12** talents and **10** cubits, which were on <u>rows forty six</u> and <u>forty seven</u> of the copper scroll. These two numbers compared to **12** priests and **10** brethren in the Book of Ezra. (Ezra 8:24)

It was notable that the priests in the Book of Ezra counted and weighted all of the gold and silver treasure, which they had brought back from Babylon and they made a written record of the details. There were the numbers **2** cubits and **20** vessels on <u>row forty eight</u> of the copper scroll and those two numbers were in the chapter of the Book of Ezra as follows: *"twenty basons of gold, of a thousand* *drams; and two vessels of fine copper, precious as gold."* (Ezra Chapter 8:27) There were **20** basons of gold and **2** vessels of fine copper. It was the only listing of the word copper in the Old Testament and it stated that it was as precious as gold. The priests had written the weights of the gold and silver treasures presumably on a scroll. Ezra was understood to be one of the main architects of completing the re-editing of the Torah. Therefore, one can only wonder, was the list of treasures that the priests had counted and weighed, later copied onto the copper scroll. The listing of *two vessels of copper* seemed to be a hint of that position?

The people then made a burnt offering of **twelve** bullocks, **ninety six** rams and **seventy seven** lambs. When the details were entered onto a spread sheet a merged number was evident as follows:

The merged number of 129,677 was evident. Obviously the number of the multiplied ages of Jared at 129,600 was the target, it being five cycles of the zodiac. However, that number was not achievable because you cannot have zero zero lambs. It was noticeable that the last three digit of that number with 677 was the same as the intercalary days in 12,960 solar years. It will be shown that the extra 77 was added in as padding to satisfy a checksum total.

Chapter 13

Infallible Numbers

There are two different features with numbers from the scripture in this chapter the first of which conducts computations with well-known biblical numbers. The second feature is to show how the biblical writers future proofed the numbers in tithe offerings in the Old Testament by encasing them in mathematical checksums.

There were particular time periods in the Bible that are associated with prophecy and they became the playground for false prophets trying to fit them in with periods in biblical history or applying them to foretell of future events. Two of those periods were with 2,300 days from the Book of Daniel and 1,260 days from the Book of Revelation. There was also the number 666 in Revelation and it is reviled because it was cited as the number of the beast. The number 666 had already featured as a checksum total on the copper scroll and the findings from this investigation will take that number out of its misery and repatriate it back to its rightful status. This investigation will now utilise those two periods of 2,300 days and 1,260 days together with the number 666 and show that the biblical scribes had utilised them to develop a theoretical formula that projected the length of the tiny time difference between the solar and the sidereal years over the period of one thousand years.

The computations were simple for when 1,260 days were multiplied by 666 and the result divided by 2,300 the outcome was 364.852174 days as shown in the equation below.

$$\frac{1{,}260 \text{ Days} \times 666}{2{,}300 \text{ Days}} = 364.852174 \text{ Days}$$

This result was just a fraction of a day short of the solar year of 365.242 days. The correlation between the result and the solar calendar year seemed to be just too close for coincidence. Because two of the numbers were obtained from the Book of Revelation, a check was carried out in the book to see if there was any information, which would shine some light on the equation. The opening lines in Chapter 9 referred to a star that fell from heaven unto the earth and to him was given the keys of the bottomless pit. A star from heaven and the earth cited in the same sentence had the hallmarks of how the sidereal and solar years were measured with respect to the reference points. In the same chapter there was the following sentence:

"Which were prepared for an hour, and a day, and a month, and a year, for to slay the third part of men." (Revelation 9:15)

The sentence listed the normal intervals of the calendar with a year, a month, a day and an hour. All that was missing was a week. However, the period of a week was cited separately in the context of 3 ½ days, which were listed twice in another chapter of the book. (Revelation 11:9, 11:11) The sentence had stated *for to slay the third part of men* and that brought to mind how Moses had three thousand men slain for worshipping the golden calf. One third of those men would be one thousand and notably, one thousand was listed six times in Revelation in the context of a thousand years. (Revelation Chapter 20)

The analysis progressed from there by multiplying the result from the equation above with 364.852174 by one thousand and the result was 364,852.174. A closer look at that number showed that it was just a little over one year short of a thousand years. The observation led to adding on the periods of one year, one month, one day and one hour from the listing, which was just quoted above. (The average length of a month in the solar calendar is 30.43 days) The result was as follows:

	364,852.174	Days
+ One Year	365.242	Days
+ One Month	30.430	Days
+ One Day	1......	Days
+ One Hour	0.042	Days

Total   365,248.888   Days

There was a remarkable result in store for when the separate listings of a week of seven days from the 3 ½ days that were listed twice in Revelation was added on to the result above, the outcome was 365,256 days, which was one thousand sidereal years. However, if the week of seven days was subtracted from the result with 365,248.888 above, the outcome was 365,242 days, which was one thousand solar years. The accuracy of the periods was extraordinary and in the realms of the paranormal at that stage of engineering development. The equation complimented the findings with the solar and sidereal years from the numbers on the copper scroll.

How meaningful however, was that theoretical equation in everyday life? The result with one thousand solar and sidereal years was of no direct importance in calendar terms. It was a theoretical model that was contrived by the mystic sage using those three biblical numbers of 1,260, 666 and 2,300. It served a purpose where it showed that the calendar periods of a year, a month, a week, a day and an hour to bridge the gap with one thousand solar and sidereal years were crafted into the equation by the sage. Just imagine the lengths the sage had to go to in order to identify the three principal numbers in that equation, which would facilitate all of those elements of the calendar in the fractional part of the computation result? How did those biblical guys ever think up that formula? What school or academy did those masters go to? It is known that the Babylonians were at the leading edge of astronomy and mathematics in the ancient world and the Jews were exiled in Babylon and that may give us an idea of where the data may have originated.

There was another aspect to this formula, which needed explaining. Multiplying the base figure of 364.852174 by one thousand was a significant part of the discovery for it was a way for the scribes to show that they knew the true lengths of the solar and sidereal years. It took the difficult fractional element of presentation into account and allowed the findings in what we know today as three decimal places to be shown in whole numbers. It meant that we could show one thousand solar years as 365,242 days and one thousand sidereal years as 365,256 days. There were no decimal fraction or Arabic numerals in biblical times but by multiplying the numbers by one thousand it catered for the fractional element in whole numbers.

That was just one function of the number 666 for it will be shown later in this chapter that it also was part of a checksum total to future proof the numbers in two sets of burnt offerings in the Book of Numbers. The period of 2,300 days will also feature again in the analysis on the dimensions of the tabernacle.

The concentration so far has mainly been on the technical details but it is important to restate the overriding factor that was likely in the minds of the prophets. Those seers wrote about a heaven out there in the abyss and that was it, words for people to believe in. But people are sceptical creatures and like Doubting Thomas, they want more than mere words to convince them that there was such a mystical dominion out there. The prophets must have envisaged that dilemma but how were they ever going to overcome the great void. This formula with solar and sidereal time was one example. It presented what effectively was seen as a gateway to the heavens in theoretical terms in much the same way as we have theorems reaching out to infinity. Therefore, the formula was a step above the written word but it does create awkward questions.

Where did the scribes get such advanced accurate knowledge of the heavens at least fifteen hundred years before the advent of mechanical clocks and telescopes? How did they ever think up that formula, which encapsulated all of the elements of the calendar? It shows the mind of a super intellect. And this was only one element of what has been unveiled in the overall research work. Therefore, when the prophets wrote of a mystical heaven in the next world, they were on the inside track on something that we still don't know about today in this advanced era of science and technology.

Mathematical Checksums

The second part of this chapter deals with mathematical checksums and how they scribes had used them to future proof important sets of numbers in the Old Testament. Those numbers on the copper scroll and in the Bible had travelled many rocky roads throughout their long journey over thousands of years. We have seen that the writers of the copper scroll had employed the use of checksums with the ages of the patriarchs to future proof the numbers. During my earlier biblical research work, I had discovered that the scribes had employed the use of checksums to future proof the validity of the numbers in parts of the Old Testament. It was therefore possible for us to evaluate if those figures in the burnt and peace offerings had retained their original values intact throughout their long rocky journey over thousands of years.

To apply a checksum, a recognisable total was required. But how were the biblical mathematicians going to provide a total for a checksum number, which would be recognisable thousands of years into the future? Those masterminds used numerical values that are the same today as they were when Daniel walked along the rivers of Babylon. The scribes pointed to the Book of Daniel with the couplet 70 and 7 from <u>rows thirty eight</u> and <u>thirty nine</u> of the scroll. Those two numbers related to a prophecy involving the periods of 70 weeks together with the period of a week. (A week of course was 7 days) A further period of 62 weeks was also involved in the prophecy. The number 62 was listed as silver talents on <u>row forty seven</u> of the scroll so it was another match. The prophecy of some event to happen in the periods of 70 and 62 weeks had evoked every oddball theory throughout the ages trying to identify when it would be fulfilled. But why had the scroll led to those numbers?

When the number 62 was multiplied by 70 the total came to 4,340. That number of 4,340 was just 7 longer than the number of days in the orbit of Jupiter. To correct the error there was a period of one week of 7 days listed with those two numbers in the Book of Daniel. The text referred to overspreading and the multiplication of 62 by 70 had overspread the orbit of Jupiter by a week of 7 days. The term overspreading led to subtracting the listed week of 7 days from the total of 4,340 and the result was the precise orbit of Jupiter at 4,333 whole days.

There was more to this puzzle however because the numbers 62 and 70 were given in weeks and not days. Because the two periods were in weeks, the orbit of Jupiter was multiplied by seven and the result was 30,331 days. It transpired that there were 135 orbits of the planet Venus in that period to with an overlap of half a week. And notably, the text in the Book of Daniel referred to the period of half a week.

The orbits of those two planets with Jupiter and Venus were utilized in checksum totals to future proof the numbers in sacrificial peace and burnt offerings in the Book of Numbers. Using the orbits of Jupiter and Venus as checksum totals was a godsend because those orbits are constants and they have the same values today as when Daniel strolled by the rivers of Babylon thousands of years ago. They were also recognizable values to readily identify.

The orbit of Jupiter is 4,332.59 days long and thus was a big number to provide a checksum total. However, the orbit of Venus is only 224.7 days long and therefore was rather small to act as a checksum total. But thirteen orbits of Venus multiply out to 2,921 days and this numbers was just one more than eight years with 365 ¼ × 8 = 2,922 days. There were also 99 lunar orbits in eight solar years. This period of eight years was very important in astronomy and it is known as the *Octaeteris*. The orbit of Jupiter and the Octaeteris of eight years of 2,922 days will be unveiled as the checksum totals that the scribes employed to futureproof the numbers in the peace and burnt offerings.

The Checksums with the Peace and Burnt Offerings

The first checksum involved adding the totals of the numbers in the twelve days offerings in Chapter 7 of the Book of Numbers to get an overall total. These totals included the optimal numbers of 1st, 2nd, 3rd day etc. together with the numbers of the plates, bowls, dishes, shekels, bullocks, rams, lambs, goats and again bullocks, rams, lambs and twelve listings of the 1st year. It also included the word both as meaning the number 2. The total came to 2,934. That number was just 12 more than the length of eight solar years of 2,922 days. The result with the checksum at 2,934 was a close call to the Octaeteris of 2,922 days but there was one aspect of the offerings which had to be considered. The 12 kids of a goat for the sin offering had a price tag on their heads. They were to be cursed with the sins of the tribes and then taken away and banished from the camp as scape goats. And when those 12 goats were taken away they would have to be deducted from the total of 2,934 thus giving an outcome of 2,922, which was the exact length of the Octaeteris. The findings proved that those numbers in the twelve days offerings of Chapter 7 of the Book of Numbers had retained their original values intact despite the rigours of the various copying processes.

The checksum result with the Octaeteris showed that the biblical intellectuals were far sighted and meticulous in their quest for perfection. That result encouraged me to check if the scribes had also inserted a checksum value to confirm if the merged numbers of 111 and 2,555 were to replace the **one, one, one** and the **two, five, five, five** numbers in the burnt and peace offerings. It meant replacing the listed numbers of animals in the burnt offerings from one bullock, one ram and one lamb with its total of 3 for each day with a total of 111. Because the concept of counting days rather than animals now applied, the listing of the 1st year relative to the animals was no longer applicable. The 2 oxen, 5 rams, 5 goats and 5 lambs had also to be replaced with a total of 2,555 for each day. Again, the listing of the 1st year with respect to the animals no longer applied and was thus omitted. The new totals for the twelve days offerings were then formed as is shown on Table 51.

Table 51: The Merged Numbers Validated by a Checksum

78	The totals of the days with 1st, 2nd, 3rd, etc. up to 12th = 78
12	Plates
12	Bowls
12	Dishes
1,560	Shekels 130 × 12 = 1,560
840	Shekels 70 × 12 = 840
120	Shekels 10 × 12 = 120
24	The word 'both' meaning 2 was cited twelve times
12	Kids of a goat
1,332	111 × 12 = 1,332
30,660	2,555 × 12 = 30,660
34,662	**Total**

When this total of 34,662 was checked out against orbital time of the planets it proved to be eight cycles of Jupiter to the very day. The totals included the 12 kids of a goat for the sin offering. That was why those goats had featured in the offerings but were later banished. It was to facilitate the first checksum with the Octaeteris of 2,922 days. However, when the goats were initially part of the offerings, their numbers were also part of this present checksum with eight orbits of Jupiter. It was a further example of the degree of perfection of those biblical masterminds in employing checksums. Thus, two seals of approval in validating that those biblical numbers had retained their original values intact had been confirmed by the use of checksums. With the original total of the offerings, it was the eight year period of the Octaeteris of 2,922 days. With the merged number version, it was eight orbits of Jupiter.

The Burnt Offering Checksum

The copper scroll had homed in on burnt offerings and in all there were eight such offerings, which comprised of bullocks, rams and lambs in that order in the Old Testament. The first checksum above had catered for the very first burnt offering and so the next checksum will apply to the remaining seven burnt offerings. It was necessary to list all the numbers of the seven burnt offerings in order to perform the checksum. The details are shown in Table 52.

Table 52: The Burnt Offerings Validation Checksum

	Bullocks	Rams	Lambs	Biblical Books
	2	1	7	Numbers Chapter 28
	2	1	7	Numbers Chapter 28
	2	1	7	Numbers Chapter 28
	1	1	7	Numbers Chapter 29
	1	1	7	Numbers Chapter 29
	1	1	7	Numbers Chapter 29
	1,000	1,000	1,000	Chronicles1 29:21
	7	7	7	Chronicles2 29:21
	70	100	200	Chronicles2 29:32
	100	200	400	Ezra 6:17
	12	96	77	Ezra 8:35
Totals	1,198	1,409	1,726	

Those totals were checked against the constants of orbital time and the following results as days were unveiled:

- 1,409 as days proved to be 16 orbits of **Mercury**.

- 1,198 + 1,726 = 2,924. This total was within two days of the Octaeteris of eight solar years. It was the second time the **Octaeteris** had been unveiled as a checksum total.

- The complete totals were 1,198 + 1,409 + 1,726 = 4,333. That result of 4,333 was the same value as one orbit of **Jupiter** to the exact whole day.

It was an incredible result to comprehend for all that was expected was possibly one checksum to give a tacit authentication to those values in the burnt offerings. In that regard, the equivalent of one orbit of Jupiter at 4,333 would have seemed sufficient to fit that purpose, for that particular numerical value alone would be a remarkable encounter. But also finding the eight year period with the Octaeteris and sixteen orbits of Mercury made the checksum truly profound. The outcome proved that those numbers in those seven burnt offerings had retained their original values intact throughout their long and rocky journey through history.

The method of encryption was a marvellous achievement for it escaped the eyes of millions over thousands of years. Because the biblical mathematicians were so far sighted I felt that they may have also encased the total of the merged numbers themselves in a checksum so that future generations would know that the merging process in creating the larger numbers with 111, 2,555, 117 and 217 was deliberately intended.

The Lost Book Found by Hilkiah in the Temple is Identified

The trail for the checksum began with the number 23 on the copper scroll and one of its matches was found in the Book of Jeremiah, which was outlined earlier. The prophet had referred to "*from the thirteenth year of Josiah, the son of Amon king of Judah, even unto this day, that is the three and twentieth year.*" (Jeremiah 25:3) Jeremiah was being very specific about listing the period of 23 years. Therefore, I had probed deeper into why Jeremiah invoked the name of Josiah.

Something unusual happened in the eighteenth year of Josiah where a lost book of Moses was found by the High Priest Hilkiah in the temple. It was referred to as the Book of the Law and when its contents were read to Josiah, he went on the rampage and destroyed the false idols in the high places of Bethel. Scholars were of the opinion the book, which was found in the temple was the Book of Deuteronomy. However, there was no real proof to verify this view. Because of finding the book, Josiah held the biggest Passover feast which had not been seen since the time of Samuel. Despite it being the feast of the Passover, the offerings did not conform to the quantity or customary type of animals, which were slaughtered at the time of Moses. Josiah gave 30,000 sheep and goats and 3,000 bullocks as his offerings. It was an enormous amount of animals which raised the question of Josiah departed from the recommended numbers on the day of the Passover as outlined by Moses?

Josiah's great grand-father Hezekiah had made burnt offerings and he also called on the people to celebrate the Passover. It seemed like a play on words where it then stated: "*It* (the Passover) *had not been celebrated in large numbers according to what was written*" (2 Chronicles 30:5) The emphasis was on *celebrated in large numbers* and could mean the large merged number of 217, which had been decoded from the Passover burnt offering in Chapter 28 of the Book of Numbers. The enormous size of the Passover offering by Josiah seemed to indicate that the larger decrypted numbers in the offerings made in the Book of Numbers may have been encased in checksums.

The merged numbers from the burnt offerings in the Book of Numbers were with three listings each of 117 and 217. There was also a burnt offering of one bullock, one ram and one lamb in Chapter 7 of the Book of Numbers and its numbers also merged to form the higher number of 111. In the same chapter, there were peace offerings which consisted of two oxen, five rams, five goats and five lambs and on the spreadsheet table the numbers merged to form the larger number of 2,555. The number 2,555 was seven years or 365 days by 7 = 2,555 days. The larger numbers in the Book of Numbers were thus 111, 2,555, 117 and 217. Those burnt offerings with the merged numbers were made back at the time of Moses and it stated that Josiah was reading from the book of Moses.

The idea of a checksum was gleaned from where Josiah's officials contributed 2,600 Passover offerings, and 300 cattle while the leaders of the Levites contributed 5,000 Passover offerings and 500 cattle. The total of those contributions came to 8,400 and that compared to the Levites share in the division of the spoils of war in Chapter 31 of the Book of Numbers. The writers had demonstrated in that chapter how a checksum was applied where the spoils of war be it sheep, cattle, donkeys or virgin women were all counted as items and distributed as one in 50 to the Levites.

Josiah had presented two groups with 3,000 bullocks and 30,000 sheep and goats and there was a particular purpose for the two groups. It was a way of having two witnesses to ensure the checksums were recognisable as legitimate. The checksums were as shown in Table 53.

Table 53: The Checksums Verify of the Merged Numbers in the Torah

	Offerings For One Day	Offerings for Remaining Days	Totals
Burnt Offering	111	111 × 11	1,221
Peace Offerimg	2,555	2,555 × 11	28,105
Burnt Offering	117	117 × 2	234
Burnt Offering	217	217 × 2	434
Total =	**3,000**	**Total =**	**29,994**

The first result at 3,000 was the exact total of one merged number each with 111, 2,555, 117 and 217 and it compared to the 3,000 bullocks that Josiah had offered. The second result at 29,994 was the totals of the remaining merged numbers with eleven times 111, eleven times 2,555, twice 117 and twice 217. There was a shortfall of six to reach the 30,000 animals bit it was too small to effect the result.

It was now evident what book Josiah had been reading. The Torah was re-edited in the general era of Josiah and all those numbers in the peace and burnt offerings were mysteriously inserted in the revised book. The new evidence indicates that Josiah had been given the PR role of launching the secretly revised Torah in the 18th year of his reign. The biblical writers displayed the covert contents of the book before our eyes by outlining the enormous Passover offering whose numbers provided the checksum totals for those vital merged numerical totals, which were in the Torah. To know about those larger merged numbers, Josiah had to have read from the revised edition of the Torah.

It was back to the matching process and we have seen how the 8,400 offerings had converted to 23 years. The number 23 was beside the number 32 on the copper scroll and when 32 was entered onto a search engine it homed in on the distribution of the spoils of war in Chapter 31 of the Book of Numbers. The spoils of war comprised of cattle, asses, sheep and virgins. Ironically, the number 32 was the Lords share of the captured virgins. The spoils were distributed by ratio and when the maths was applied, the total came to 840 for the Lord. The trail was an eye opener for the Levites share came to 8,400. It was the same number as the totals of the Passover offerings that were made by the Levites at the time of Josiah.

The reason why the trail had led to the 8,400 in the spoils of war was now obvious. The distribution of the spoils was an exercise in adding up the numbers of the captured booty into a grand checksum total irrespective if they were virgins, sheep, asses or cattle. Their total became neutral numbers. We saw the earlier checksum findings and here the scribes had left us this practical example of how to create such a checksum total and importantly, the totals were identified with 8,400 which as days converted to 23 years. The time period prepared the way to use the time periods with the orbits of the planets as recognizable checksums totals.

Chapter 14

The Cosmic Tabernacle

The next part of the matching process led to the tabernacle in the Book of Exodus. The tabernacle was one of the most holy shrines of Hebrew worship. This transportable temple comprised of a tent, which was divided into two rooms by a veil. One room was God's Holy of Holies chamber and it symbolized heaven. It housed the Ark of the Covenant, God's throne and two angelic cherubim. Only the high priest could enter into the holy of holies chamber and that was just once a year on the Day of Atonement. The second room in the tent was known as the Holy Place and in it were a table, incense altar and candlesticks. It was in the holy place where the regular priests ministered and it symbolized this earthly world. There was a perimeter fence around the tent and it was built with pillars and curtains. At the entrance to the tent there was a brass burnt offering altar.

The matching exercise that led to the tabernacle began with the 70 talents and 10 talents on the scroll and the couplet had compared to 70 shekels of silver and 10 shekels of gold in the tithe offering of Chapter 7 of the Book of Numbers. When the twelve days of offerings were made, their totals were listed at the end of the chapter with 70 talents and 2,400 shekels. On checking to find another appearance of the number 70 in the Old Testament, the search engine stopped in the Book of Exodus where 70 talents and 2,400 shekels of bronze were used in the construction of the tabernacle. (Exodus 38:24-29) This was the third time in the matching process of finding a pair of numbers together in the Old Testament and then using them in a matching process.

The first indication of something worthy of investigation was with the three donations of treasures to build the tabernacle. Those treasures were listed as 29 talents and 730 shekels of gold, 100 talents and 1,775 shekels of silver and 70 talents and 2,400 shekels of bronze. It was noticeable that three out of the four listings of talents and shekels for the gold and silver weights equated to orbital time periods. The number 29 equated to the lunar month, 730 to two solar years of 365 + 365 days and 1,775 equated to five lunar years. It was from one treasure trail with the copper scroll to another treasure trail with the gold and silver that was used to decorate the tabernacle.

Finding the cosmic data in the gold and silver numerical weights to decorate the tabernacle led to an examination of the materials and completed structure to see if there was evidence of more time periods. The instructions and measurements to build the tabernacle were listed twice in the Book of Exodus. There was one peculiar omission however, where no size was listed for the tabernacle tent. It meant that the size of the tent had to be determined. It transpired that the various biblical institutions that I referenced had worked out a large size for the tabernacle tent and it was 30 cubits long by 10 cubits wide by 10 cubits high. However, Professor Richard Friedman had worked out a small tent size which was 20 cubits long, 8 cubits wide and 10 cubits high. (Friedman p 181) The analysis was conducted using both tent sizes with a remarkable outcome. It was found that the various dimensions in square cubits had the same numerical values as the orbits of the planets together with other related cycle when the small tent was utilised. In all, fourteen time periods were detected with the small tent size but there were no orbits detected when the larger tent was utilised.

The biblical writers had given a clear indication that there were time periods overlaid on the tabernacle where they referred to the holy sanctuary having being trodden underfoot for 2,300 days. (Daniel 8:13, 14) It transpired in the investigation, that the surface areas of the tabernacle tent and the perimeter fence came to 2,300 square cubits. From the findings above, it indicated that the square cubits equated to 2,300 days as was implied in the Book of Daniel.

At first, it seemed that the designers of the tabernacle had zealously taken *the gate of heaven* aspect to the extreme when they factored in the orbits of the planets into its dimensions. However, the findings have identified that it was to do with the traditional ceremonial worship at the tabernacle. The High Priest came to the tabernacle once a year on the Day of Atonement and the evidence suggested that this visit was at the rising of the sun. It outlined about this yearly visit in the Book of Hebrews where it stated *"as the high priest entereth into the holy place every year with blood of others;"* (Hebrews 9:25) The Bible did outline the duties the high priests performed in the tabernacle but it was a very limited view of what was enacted behind the scenes.

The entrance to the tabernacle was to face east towards the rising of the sun. This would have caused a dazzling effect with the rising sun lighting up the two chambers of the structure. It would have been like a brilliant flash of lightning when the sun reflected on the gold plated walls and the golden ark and other golden furniture. There was also the reflection from women's looking glasses, which were hung on the external bronze altar. (Exodus 38:8)

The step by step approach to the tabernacle ritual by the High Priest on the Day of Atonement will now be outlined to show how the orbits of the planets were unveiled. He would have withdrawn the entrance curtain of the perimeter fence and then the entrance curtain to the tent and then the dividing veil to the inner chamber. That was the transfiguration moment of the ritual, because it would have seen a dazzling display of light from the rising sun reflect on the golden walls and ornaments and from the women's looking glasses. The evidence suggests that it was an earthly demonstration of light overcoming darkness and it mirrored the conjunctions of Mercury and Venus in the heavens when they came in out of the abyss of the night sky to be purified when they crossed the face of the sun.

The religious ethos was to let in the light and the rising sun would have fulfilled that mission as the High Priest opened the curtains on the Day of Atonement. The tabernacle structure was static but the sunshine and its reflections were a moving source of light, which would have created various permutations and combinations on the visible surface areas where the orbits and cycles of the planets were overlaid. In that way, the planets overlaid on the tabernacle dimensions would be purified by the light of the rising sun.

1. The High Priest would have withdrawn the entrance curtain of the fence and the sun would have shone on the tent entrance curtain and the group of six curtains at either side towards the front with its total of 344 square cubits equating to the long-term cycle of Jupiter at 344 years.

2. He would then have withdrew the entrance curtain to the tent and the remaining external surface areas of the visible tent fabrics and the perimeter fence was 2,160 square cubits, which equated to one constellation of the zodiac at 2,160 Years.

3. At the same time, the surface areas of the holy place without the entrance curtain plus the table and incense altar was 383 square cubits, which equated to the long-term cycle of Saturn at 383 Years as shown in the image below.

The Long-term Cycle of Saturn at 383 Years

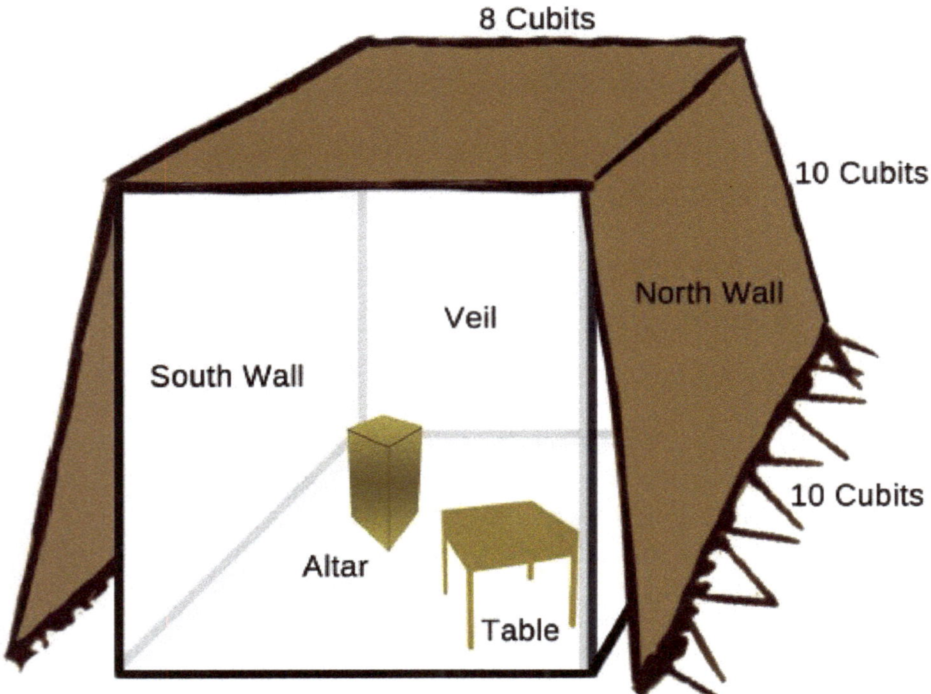

4. In the same picture, the sun would have also shone on the square areas of the perimeter fence and external brass altar together with the square areas of the holy outer chamber room, incense altar and table and their total at 5,108 square cubits equated to two periods of seven years with just two days of a shortfall as shown in the image below.

The Period of 5,108 Days in the Square Areas of Perimeter, Outer Room and Furniture

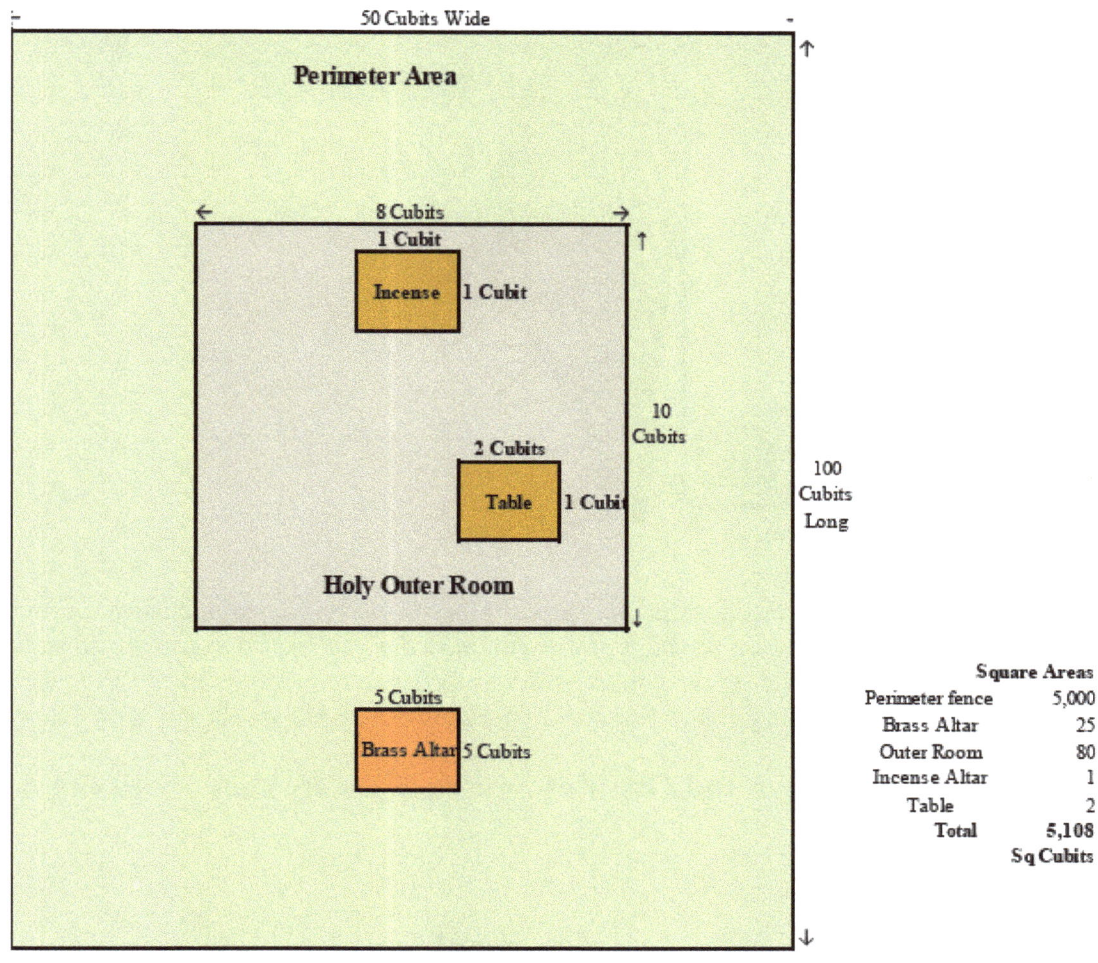

5. The high priest would then have removed the dividing veil and the remaining internal surface areas of the tent and the ark, mercy seat, table, incense altar and breast plate was 686.5 square cubits, which equated to the orbit of Mars as shown in the image below.

The Orbit of Mars in the Surface areas of the Tabernacle Tent and its Furniture

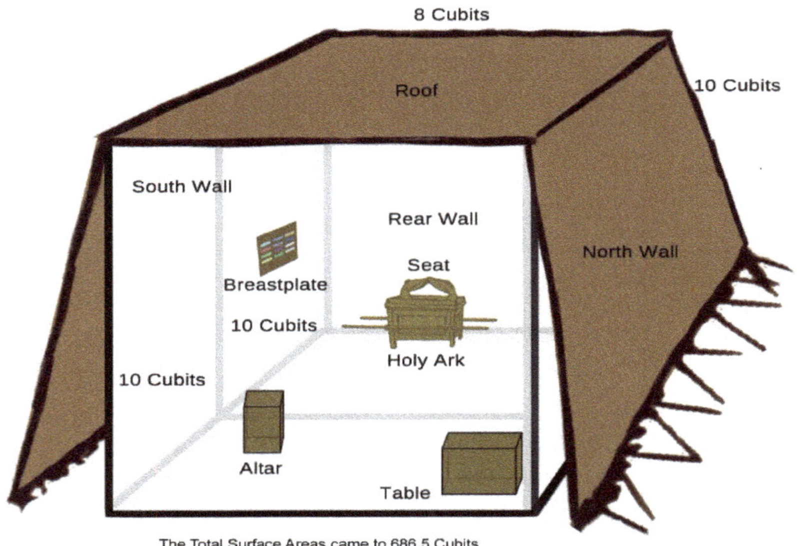

6. It specifically stated in the Book of Exodus that the incense altar was to be placed in close proximity to the Ark of the Covenant. Therefore, when the high priest withdrew the veil their two surface areas were close together and they added up to 29.5 square cubits. This was the same numbers as the 29.53 Days in a lunar month and the 29.45 Years for the Orbit of Mercury. The ark and the altar are shown in the diagram.

The Lunar Month of 29.5 Days and Orbit of Saturn at 29.45 Years with the Ark and Altar

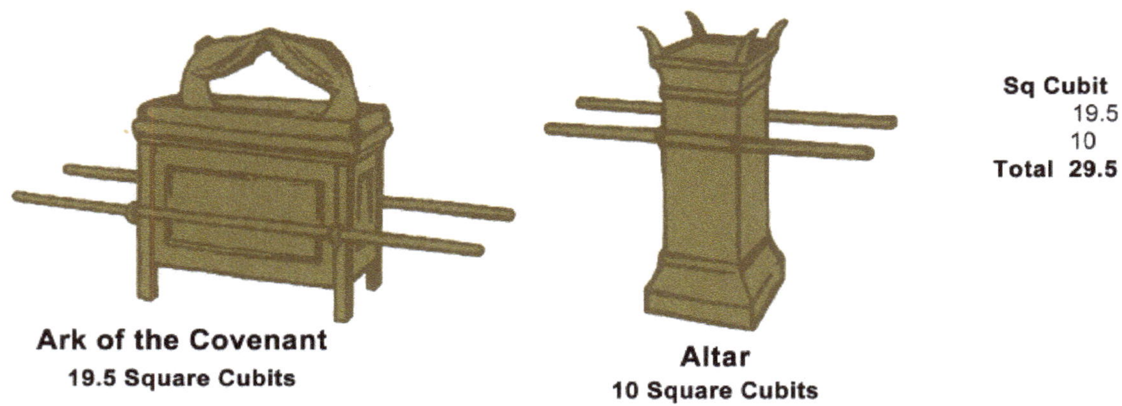

7. At the same time, the sun would have shone on the fifteen bars coated with gold and their surface areas was 225 square cubits, which equated to the orbit of Venus at 225 days.

8. The high priest then would have stepped into the holy of holies and the square areas of the chamber plus the square areas of the ark, mercy seat and breastplate was 87.75 square cubits, which equated to the orbit of Mercury at 88 days.

The Orbit of Mercury in the Square Areas of the Holiest Chamber and its Furniture

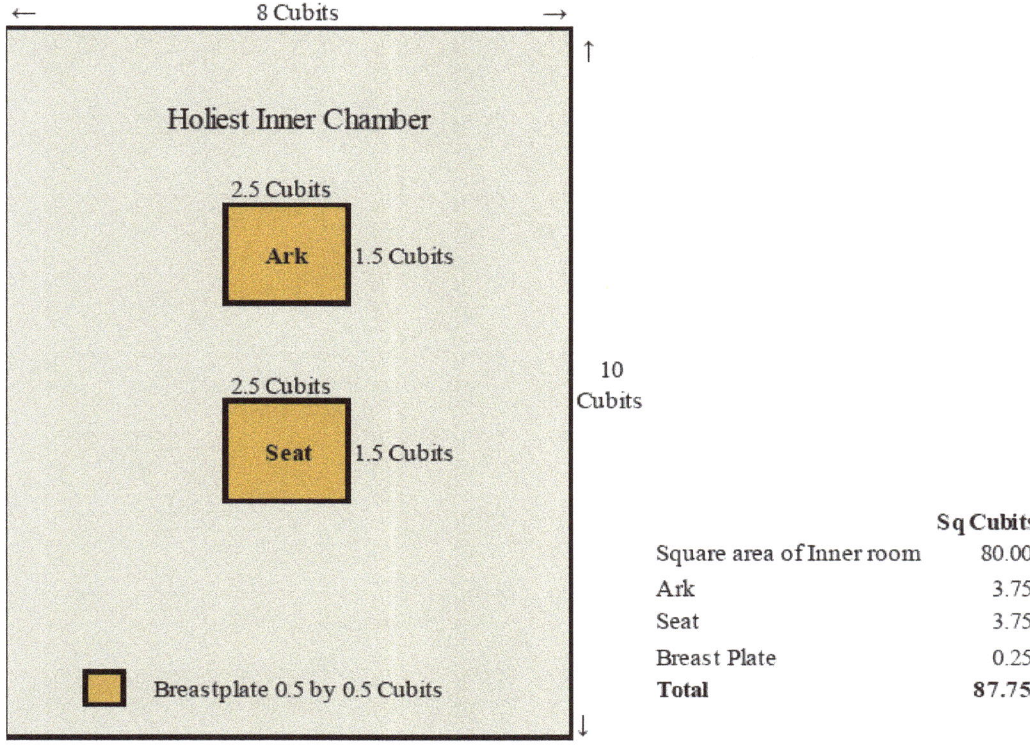

Total = 87.75 Square Cubits

9. At the same time, the sun would have also shone on the remaining surface areas of the inside of the tent and on the mercy seat, table, incense altar, external burnt offering altar and the breastplate with its total of 777 square cubits, which equated to the long-term cycle of Venus at 777 years.

10. The high priest would then have placed the veil over the Ark of the Covenant in conformity with what Moses did when he erected the tabernacle. (Exodus 40:3) It resulted where the surface areas of the walls and ceiling of the inner holy of holies chamber together with the seat and breastplate added up to 364 square cubits, which equated to the number of days in of the biblical solar calendar year.

The Solar Year in the Surface Areas of the Holiest Chamber, Seat and Breastplate

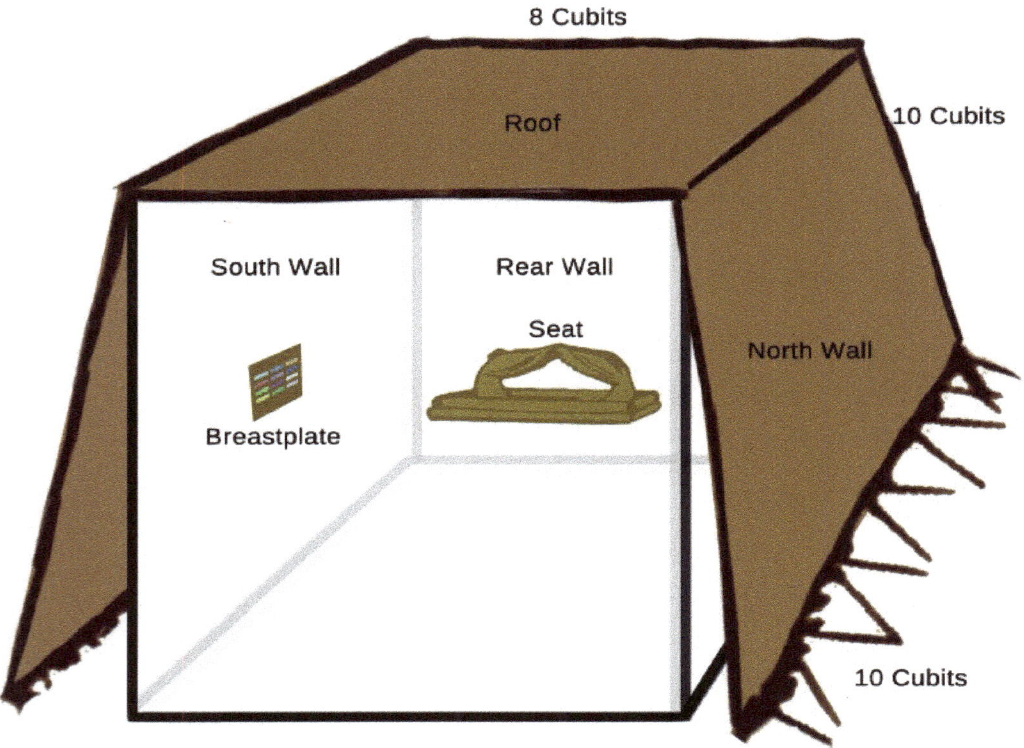

The Total Surface Areas came to 364 Square Cubits

Those ten snapshots of the planets in the dimensions of the tabernacle at the rising of the sun were symbolised by the transfiguration of Christ and that was indicated when Peter said let us build three tabernacles.

The pilgrimage had begun by pulling back the perimeter fence curtain at the rising of the sun and followed the shining beam of light as it brought the planets formations etched into the areas of the tabernacle to life and remarkably, it ended with the solar year in the holy of holies chamber.

Chapter 15

The Messiah Timeline

It was shown earlier that the period of 117 years was the sum total of the reigns of Hezekiah, Manasseh, Amon and Josiah. During the reign of King Josiah, something unusual happened in his 18th year on the throne where a long lost book of Moses was found in Solomons temple. It was reckoned that the king's 18th year was around 618 BCE. Taking that arrangement with 117 years as an intended prompt, it was decided to date back in time from Josiah in 618 BCE, using the three periods of 117 years that were decoded from the burnt offerings in Chapter 29 of the Book of Numbers. It dated back in time to the year 969 BCE, which was reckoned to be the year that Solomon was crowned king.

The dating back in time continued using the three decrypted periods of 217 years that were decoded from the burnt offerings in Chapter 28 of the Book of Numbers and they led back from Solomon in 969/70 BCE to 1,620 BCE. However, there was no important event that could be attributed to that year. Those three periods of 217 years were also applied to date forward in time from Josiah in 618 BCE and it ended in the year 33 CE using the astronomical dating method. (It should be noted that the conventional calendar had no year zero for it started in the year 1 CE and dated back in time from 1 BCE. Therefore, I have used the astronomical method of dating which allows for having a year zero.) It was an astonishing finding because it is reckoned that 33 CE was the year that Jesus was crucified. There was a tantalising surprise in store where the length of time from 1,620 BCE to when Jesus died in 33 CE proved to be 777 days by 777 times. That remarkable timeline was the ultimate with all the sevens and it adorned the whole sweep of biblical history.

The investigation now moves on to outline how a second method was uncovered and it ran in parallel with the 777 days by 777 times timeline.

The Days of a Solar Calendar Paraded as Men in Two Censuses

Many years before I came across the copper scroll, I had made a remarkable discovery with the numbers that were supposed to be two censuses of the twelve tribes of Israel. It was necessary to outline this discovery now because it has an impact on the copper scroll calendar timeline. It was obvious that the scribes had pointed to the tribes of Israel with couples of numbers on the copper scroll. In the matching process, the couplet with 40 and 42 on Rows 5 and 6 of the copper scroll led to the 42 stops the Israelites made during their 40 years in the desert wilderness. On Row 21, there were the numbers 1 and 12 and there were one tribe with the Levits together with the twelve tribes of Israel.

But the matches with those four numbers of 40 and 42 together with 1 and 12 were in general terms and did not home in on the censuses. Therefore, the matching exercise continued to see if the scribes had strategically pointed to the two censuses of the tribes of Israel. It was found that the couplet with **9** and **20** led to the only listing of those two numbers together in the Old Testament and it was in the Book of Samuel. It was there that King David instructed the captain of the host, Joab, to go through all the tribes of Israel and number the people. Joab's reply was rather telling where it stated: *"Now the lord thy God add unto the people. How many so ever they be, an hundredfold, and* *that the eyes of my lord the king may see it;"* It took the period of **9** months and **20** days to hold the census, which were the same two numbers on the copper scroll.

The story was repeated in the first Book of Chronicles where Joab's response to the king was equally telling as follows: *The lord made his people an hundred times so many more as they be:"* The two statements from Joab were very distinct and showed that the scribes of the copper scroll had wanted future investigators to know that the censuses were multiplied by one hundred. The copper scroll had led to the period of 9 months and 20 days to conduct the census. Therefore, it was prudent to introduce the discovery I made previously with two censuses of those twelve tribes.

Jacob who was also called Israel, had twelve sons by two wives and two handmaidens, who were named Leigh, Rachel, Zilpah and Bilah. At the time of a severe famine, Jacob and his family went to live in Egypt where his son Joseph had risen to be second in command of the kingdom. The Bible tells us that after 430 years of living in Egypt, Moses led the descendants of Israel out of bondage and into the desert wilderness.

The first census was held by Moses after the first year of the exodus out of Egypt and the total came to 603,550 men. That was an enormous size of a population especially as there were only seventy in Jacobs family when they went to live in Egypt just seven generation previously. One could see immediately that they were not the totals of a census, because eleven of the numbers ended with a double zero whereas a normal tally would end with the numbers from 0 up to 9. The double zero indicated that the census had been multiplied by one hundred and that accounted for the   enormous sizes of the tally.

Without the clothing of the double zero, the numbers of the tribes were laid bare because it was plain to see that the total of men with the tribe of Benjamin at 354 compared to the days in a lunar year. The revelations continued where the numbers of Leah's five sons in the first census added up to 2,922, which were the number of days in the Octaeteris of eight years. A pattern was developing where the numbers of the tribes were equating to time periods in days and it continued where the Levite tribe was counted separately but their total must rate as the biggest blunder in the Bible. The Levites were broken up into three groups when they were counted in the first census with the descendants of Levi's three sons Gershom, Kohath and Merari. The number of descendants a month old or more for each son was 7,500, 8,600 and 6,200 and the total was given as 22,000. It must rate as the biggest numerical mistake in the Old Testament because the sum of those three numbers actually came to a total of 22,300. There was a purpose for that blunder for it introduced a formula to utilise what were paraded as the numbers of a tribe as days and convert them to solar years as outlined in Appendix 1.

The second census was held at the end of the forty years in the wilderness when all but two of the men from the first census had died. Again, eleven of the twelve totals ended with a double zero as if they had been multiplied by one hundred. There were also blatant anomalies where the totals for Gad in the second census were the same as for Ephraim in the first census. It was the same where the total for Asher in the second census were the same as for Naphtali in the firsts census.

Those two anomalies led me to add the numbers of the twelve tribes in the first census to the numbers of the twelve tribes in the second census and then halve the twelve totals to get the average values. There archived behind those simply calculations, lay one of the most profound secrets in the Bible. To begin with, the average total for the tribe of Ephraim was 36,500 and that without the double zero was the number of days in a solar year. It was the biblical imperative of a third witness to confirm that each man in the census represented a solar day. There was another blatant anomaly where the number for Benjamin in that inner chart was the same as for Ephraim in the alleged first census and for Gad in the alleged second census.

The revelations continued where the total of the first seven tribes in sequence From Reuben down to Manasseh in the inner chart added up to 365,240 days, which was within two days of 1,000 solar years. It just needed two extra men to represent two days and the biblical writers had arranged for that correction where it outlined that Joshua and Caleb were the only two men who had survived from the alleged first census. That brought the number up to 365,242, which was exactly the number of days in 1,000 solar years and it therefore, was a very reliable fourth witness. The fifth witness was where the total of the next two tribes in sequence with Ephrim and Benjamin added up to 77,000 days, which converted to 210 years 299 days. That period compared to the 210 years the Israelites spent in Egypt as outlined in the Book of Jasher.

The analysis continued and it was found that the totals of the numbers for Ephraim, Benjamin, Asher and Naphtali in the inner chart added up 173,850 days and it converted to 476 years to within five days. It was an astounding result because the period of 476 years was the time given from the exodus out of Egypt to when Solomon became king. I.e., Solomon started to build the temple in the fourth year of his reign, which was 480 years after the exodus. (480 – 4 = 476 years) Those four tribes were not in sequence but the scribes had catered for that obstacle so that they could be arranged in sequence together. It was the sixth witness to confirm that the men in the censuses represented the days of a solar calendar. The total of what were paraded as men came to 602,640 days and it converted to 1,650 years to within nine days.

The next step was to overlay this solar calendar on biblical history and the pivotal point was with Solomon because of the 476 years from the time of the exodus to when he was crowned king. It was reckoned that Solomon became king in 969 or 970 BCE and from there, the solar timeline dated back by 476 years to the exodus in 1,445/6 BCE. The extra segment on the timeline continued on to 1,620 BCE, which was the same year that had been pinpointed by the copper scroll timeline. Therefore, something major must have occurred in that year and it would have to become part of the investigation.

The solar calendar timeline was then cast forward in time by one thousand years from Solomon in 969/70 BCE and it led to what we now know as 29 CE using the astronomical dating method. That year was recognisable where it stated in Luke's gospel that John the Baptist began to preach in the 15th Year of the rule of Tiberius. It is reckoned by historians that the 15th year of Tiberius was the year 29 CE. Jesus was six months younger than John and Luke tells us that his ministry began when he was about thirty years of age. By applying the Roman dynastic reckoning for calculating the 15th year of Tiberius and adding on the extra six months for Jesus, it brought the dating to the year 30 CE. That was the year when Jesus began to preach.

Two Genealogies

The investigation then focused the attention to find out if there was a significant event that happened in 1,620 BCE. This led the investigation to two genealogies one of which was in Matthew's Gospel and the other in Luke's gospel. The genealogy in Matthew's gospel outlined that there were 42 generations from Abraham down to Jesus and it listed the men of each generation. In Luke's gospel, it listed the men in 56 generations from Jesus back to Abraham with the exception of three men who had been omitted. It was impossible to date the time period from Abraham to Jesus and Vise Versa, because many of the ages of the men in each generation were not listed in the Bible.

This was where the 777 day by 777 times timeline and the solar calendar timeline were invaluable because they could be overlaid on those two genealogies. By doing so, it would date the epochs of the Bible. This method would result with a different average age for each man in each of the genealogies. The outcome showed that the set age in in Matthew's genealogy was forty years for each generation and it was thirty years in Luke's genealogy for each generation. A set age for each man in a genealogy may appear to be a very strange way to date history, but it was a method used by the Greeks to date history with their line of monarchs.

The outcome of dating with different set ages in each of the genealogies was sensational, because the periods of forty years and thirty years were like cliches in the Bible. King David and his son Solomon both reigned for forty years and it also applied to many more leaders in the Old Testament. The 42 stops by the Israelites during their 40 years in the wilderness therefore, was like a dress rehearsal blueprint for the 42 generations of 40 years in Matthew's genealogy.

It was likewise with the period of thirty years, where it stated in Luke's gospel that Jesus was about thirty when he began his ministry. The Levite priests were also thirty years of age when they began their ministry and three of Noah's descendant were thirty years when they became fathers. Finally, there was a template for those two period of forty and thirty years with the two genealogies and it was with King David who was thirty years old when he became King and he ruled for forty years.

By overlaying the copper scroll calendar and the solar calendar on those two genealogies, it solved the mystery of what happened in the year 1,620 BCE. It was the year that Isaac was born. Both secret timelines had therefore began at the birth of Isaac in 1,620 BCE. With the solar calendar timeline, it pinpointed the year of the exodus and when Solomon was crowned king in 969/70 BCE to stop at the thirty year old Jesus in 30 CE. In turn, the copper scroll calendar timeline went from the birth of Isaac to the year that Solomon was crowned king in 969/70 BCE and onto Josiah in 618 BCE, then onto 33 CE when Jesus was crucified. In reality, there was one timeline but two different methods to map it out from Isaac down to Jesus. The timeline is shown in Illustration 8 and it seemed preordained that it should be called – The Messiah Timeline.

Illustration 8: The Messiah Timeline

A	Years	← 217 + 217 + 217 Years →	← 117 + 117 + 117 →	← 217 + 217 + 217 Years →		
B	Days	←------------------ 777 Days by 777 Times ------------------→				
C	Dates	33 CE	30 CE	618 BCE	969/70 BCE	1,445/6 BCE	1,620 BCE
C	Names	Jesus	Josiah	Solomon	Exodus	Isaac
D	Years	←3 Years→	←------- 365,242 Days or 1,000 Years -------→	← 476 Years →	←------------→

The details of the Messiah timeline are as follows:

A. The timeline outlined in green with three periods each of 117 and 217 years back in time from Josiah in 618 BCE to Solomon in 969/70 BCE and then to Isaac in 1,620 BCE. There were also three periods of 217 years forward in time from Josiah down to Jesus in 33 CE. Those periods all added up to 1,653 years.

B. The 777 days by 777 times period in days is shown in green and it was just under seventeen intercalary days short of 1,653 years.

C. Our conventional calendar dating method is outlined in C and it lists the pertinent years with Isaac, the Exodus, Solomon, Josiah and Jesus. Because there was no year zero in the Julian/Gregorian calendar, the dating was corrected by using the more precise astronomical dating.

D. The solar calendar periods are shown in gold colour and it also ran from Isaac in 1,620 BCE to the exodus in 1,445 BCE and onto Solomon in 969/70 BCE to end with the thirty year old Jesus in 30 CE. It was reckoned that Jesus preached for three years and that brought the solar calendar method up to 33 CE.

It was immaculate how the two methods to map out the time line were like a mirror image of each other in showing Isaac in 1,620 BCE, Solomon in 969/70 BCE and Jesus from 30 to 33 CE. The 777 days by 777 times period was short of 1,653 years by just over sixteen intercalary days. Another revelation was in store, because those intercalary days would have been fulfilled at the end of the timeline where Jesus died on the eve of the 14th day to the Passover and by his three days in the tomb.

Thus, there was the biblical imperative of two methods to map out the Messiah timeline. Because the copper scroll calendar dated from the time of Josiah in 618 BCE, it would suggest that it was in that era when the timeline was devised possibly by the priestly writer known as P. Dating back to Solomon and onto 1,620 BCE with Isaac would seem to have been a theoretical exercise. It did not mean that Isaac lived in that era, but that would not have mattered as he was now fulfilling a mission that would give rise to the prophets. It was in that era from King Hezekiah to Josiah and onto Ezra that the predictions of a Messiah took hold and the idea of a mystical heaven in the afterlife was fostered.

From Josiah in 618 BCE, it would have been possible to count the days of the Messiah timeline forward in time and have it as a divine mission for the elite priesthood. Finally at *the end of days,* the reed featured as follows:

And about the ninth hour Jesus cried with a loud voice, saying, Eli, Eli, lama sabachthani? That is to say, My God, my God, why hast thou forsaken me? Some of them that stood there, when they heard that, said, this man calleth for Elias. And straightway one of them ran, and took a sponge, and filled it with vinegar, and put it on a reed, and gave him to drink. (Matthew 27:47- 48)

The detractor put the sponge on a reed and gave it to Jesus to drink. The reed for measuring the Messiah timeline had thus prevailed right up to the final breath of Jesus. There was a special seven year conjunction of Mercury in the year 33 CE and a partial lunar eclipse on Friday 3rd April of the same year and from analysis of the tabernacle, the evidence suggests that was the date and year of the crucifixion of Jesus.

This was just a snapshot of the Messiah timeline but it gives a purpose for why the Torah was re-edited and the burnt offerings inserted. The full details of this timeline are outlined by the author in a book entitled: *The Messiah Immortalised in Time* as shown in the Bibliography.

Conclusion

The Bible had endured for thousands of years before it crash landed to scientific determinism. The almighty power of the inspired word had finally proved inadequate to match the relentless stream of scientific revelations, which explained in theoretical or technical terms, mysteries that were once seen as miraculous wonders or terrible omens. This enlightenment has seen the faithful shout louder to defend their threatened territory. But words were no match against the unyielding superiority of a medium, which was based on the language of science, numbers and mathematics. It seemed that the magic and mysticism of those ancient biblical times had lost their enchanting appeal. Then a copper scroll was found in a cave by the Dead Sea and it was a vessel to carry scientific data of astronomy from the biblical intelligentsia through the harsh elements of time and space.

The scribes had consigned the sacred 777 day calendar indices together with the data on the planets onto expensive copper in the expectation that the metal would endure longer than papyrus or animal hides. To further safeguard the precious data, the scribes pretended the numbers were weights of gold and silver treasures knowing that whoever found the copper scroll, would protect it with zeal hoping to find the buried valuables. Almost two thousand years went by and the copper became oxidised and brittle. Imagine if a nomadic treasure hunter had found the scroll and tried to unroll the sheets of copper? Thankfully, the finder was an archaeologist and he carefully handled the oxidised copper knowing that it would disintegrate if the pieces were unrolled.

The copper scroll remained an enigma for over sixty years because the list of vast treasures confounded biblical scholars. Unfortunately, nobody asked the obvious questions about its presentation with numbers. For instance, why was there a need to be so precise about how many cubits to dig to locate exact weights of gold and silver talents? All it needed was to give an indication where the gold and silver bullion was buried and that would have been sufficient allurement for determined treasure hunters to grab their spades. The absence of cubits and numerical weights of treasures at many of those sites suggested that those cubits and treasure weights at the other sites were superfluous or perhaps may have served an alternative purpose.

The initial evidence to show that the copper scroll contained intelligent data were with the numbers to form pi and a circle together with Enoch's solar calendar. A carefully arranged structure was then identified with those Greek letters acting as brackets to form groups for some of the checksum totals with the ages of the patriarchs. But the principal function of the Greek letters was with forming the indices of the 777 day calendar. By adding up the numbers between the various sets of Greek letters or combinations thereof, the totals formed five periods in years and nineteen intercalary days of the calendar indices.

It was outlined in the Introduction that there were references to a secret sealed scroll or book in the Books of Isaiah, Daniel and Revelation, which nobody could read. It appeared relative to this investigation with the copper scroll, where the prophet Isaiah wrote as follows: *Now go, write it before them in a table, and note it on a scroll, that it may be for the time to come for ever and ever:* (Isaiah 30:8) It was fitting because the numbers on the copper scroll had to be written on a table and the words noted on a scroll. Furthermore, the periods in the calendar timetable on the copper scroll were about a time to come for ever and ever.

Isaiah clarified the issue in the same chapter where he also wrote: *Ye shall defile also the covering of thy graven images of silver, and the ornament of thy molten images of gold: thou shalt cast them away as a menstruous cloth;* (Isaiah 30:22) Just as Isaiah had outlined, the defiling treasures of gold and silver were cast aside when the numbers on the copper scroll were seen to be significant.

The menstruous cloth introduced the menstrual cycle and ancient cultures associated that cycle with the lunar month. Isaiah again had his finger on the pulse where just a few versus down he stated: *that the light of the moon shall be the light of the sun and the light of the sun shall be sevenfold, as the light of seven days.* It proclaimed the lunar and solar time, which lay within the numerical facade. The reference to sevenfold was pertinent because there were the periods of 7, 777, 777 + 777 and 7,777 years together with 777 × 777 days on the copper scroll. That was six periods and Isaiah had made it sevenfold with the reference to the remaining period of 7 days. The evidence indicated that the mysterious sealed scroll and the encrypted copper scroll were the same document especially as nobody could read them.

It can now be seen why it stated in the Book of Genesis that Enoch walked with God who took him. In his dream travels through the heaven's, it stated that he was shown the heavenly tablets. Because of the significant role that can be attributed to Enoch relative to the formation of the tables of astronomy, it would indicate that the copper scroll matrix of numbers were those tablets. To support this observation, there was a reference in the Book of Enoch to the son of man as head of days as follows: *"And who revealeth all the treasures of that which is hidden."* (The Parables Chapter 46 2) All of the treasures which is hidden was like a dictionary description of the copper scroll with its hidden treasures.

It is interesting to try and identify how the biblical timekeepers had acquired the knowledge on the planets and the calendar timetable. Because some of the long-term cycles of the planets were found on a Babylonian tablet, it indicated that the data on the planets originated from that kingdom. The periods of 3,000, 6,000 and 12,000 years were in the calendar timetable and they were the same periods as were in the Zoroastrian time of the long dominion with four quadrants of 3,000 years adding up to 12,000 years. Therefore, it indicates that these particular periods in the calendar timetable had originated with the Persians.

The two strands of evidence with the origins of the planetary data on astronomy and the Zoroastrian time of the long dominion were acquired by the biblical writers most likely at the time of the exile in Babylon. There was also a third strand of evidence, which dated to that era and it was when the ages of the first patriarchs were covertly inserted in the Torah. Those ages had proved to be the checksum totals on the copper scroll and the number 777 with Lamech was the yardstick of the calendar timetable. Friedman reckoned that it was the Redactor R who inserted the ages of the first patriarchs in the Book of Genesis and that was at the time of Ezra, which was around 500 BCE.[14]

The connection with Ezra continued where it outlined in Chapter 8 of the Book of Ezra that the priests weighted all of the gold and silver together with the vessels, which they had brought back from Babylon. We were led to believe that weighing the gold and silver also happened with the treasures on the copper scroll but it was very strange that the weight of every item was listed very precisely. Among those treasures that were weighed were two vessels of fine copper, precious as gold. (Ezra 8:27) It was the only listing of the word copper in the KJV version of the Old Testament. The wording was also very explicit in Ezra about recording the weights of treasures as follows: *"By number and by weight of every one: and all the weight was written at that time."* (Ezra 8:34) By number and by weight all the weights of treasures were written at that time and that was similar to how the treasures were written on the copper scroll.

Some of the intercalary days of the calendar timetable were the same as the numbers of exiles who returned from Babylon with Nebo at 52 and Magbish at 156 and Elam at 1,254. (Ezra Chapter 2) Those were the same numbers as the intercalary days in 1,000, 3,000 and 24,000 solar years. To

---

[14] Richard Elliot Friedman, *Who Wrote the Bible*, (Harper Publishers, 1997). 223-233. 246.

have three numbers in sequence that matched three of the intercalary day periods in the calendar timetable was the biblical standard of three witnesses to justify it was intended.

The calendar timetable periods were detected in the dimensions of the tabernacle and that icon can be traced back to the writer P who re-edited the Torah. It was also P who inserted the two censuses of the tribes of Israel whose numbers were shown to be the days of a solar calendar, which formed the Messiah timeline. The Redactor R also had a hand in preserving the sacred data because it was he who inserted the burnt offerings in Chapters 28 and 29 of the Book of Numbers where more of the calendar time periods were covertly encrypted.[15]

The top ten matches were displayed and they showed that couplets of numbers and large single numbers on the copper scroll were targeting the Old Testament. One of the matches revealed that the 600 talents with vessels of gold and silver from the scroll compared to 600 listings of the words *gold* and *silver* in the Old Testament. That was a miraculous match to encounter because the Hebrew Bible set of books would have undergone many phases of copying over the centuries with the possibility of acquiring errors in the process. There was also the translation to the English version with the KJV in 1611 and it could be expected that there may have also been errors in that process. The 600 talents on the copper scroll had also a second function where it matched up with the only listing of 600 talents in the Bible. That listing was divine for it was the 600 talents of gold that was overlaid on the holy of holies house in Solomon's temple. The temple was the centre of attraction and it produced another match made in heaven. The total of the cubits listed to build the temple in Chapter 7 of the first Book of Kings were 386.5 cubits and this total compared exactly with the 386.5 cubits that were listed on the copper scroll. The various matches with a large number or pairs of numbers had targeted their counterparts in the Old Testament and identified the good book as the duplicate inventory.

The calendar periods on the copper scroll were instrumental in identifying the Messiah timeline which ran like a spine through the Bible from Abraham down to Jesus. It was a virtual timeline that was paralleled by the solar calendar periods. By overlaying this twin-track timeline on Matthew's and Luke's genealogies, it identified that the periods of forty and thirty years respectively pertained to each man in the generations. The elite circle of priests had never divulged the existence of this sacred timeline to the fraternity but now it changes the whole perception of the predictions relating to a Messiah. It shows that the coming of a Messiah involved the biggest planning exercise ever enacted and it was delivered with precision. Not only was Jesus in the right place Bethlehem as foretold by the prophets, but he was also there to the very years of 30 to 33 CE as revealed by the twin-track timeline.

The written text of scripture is held to be the divine word of God and above reproach by devout worshippers. Unfortunately, the same was not true for the numbers in the Bible and so the God of the ancient Hebrew's was inadvertently placed in the position of been treated as numerically suspect. It meant that a huge portion of the Bible was glossed over because it was professionally risky for academics to get involved with what appeared to be hosts of ridiculed inflated numbers. The Bible focused on a heavenly dominion, which was invisible to mere mortals. It was ironic therefore, how the facts and figures of the heavens in the Bible were also invisible to the devoted fold. Thus, centuries of sermons and lectures about the keys to the kingdom of heaven were no more than hollow homilies, because the algorithms to illuminate the gateways to that celestial lighthouse never featured.

Biblical scholarship is built on large bibliographies in order to justify and advance the validity of an opinion. But many of those references that were quoted from the works of previous academics were themselves suspect, because the writers were operating in a vacuum. They were oblivious to

---

[15] Richard Elliot Friedman p 250-254.

the archives of cosmic knowledge in the Bible. Why had nobody over the centuries in biblical schools found that the dimensions of the tabernacle had the same numerical values as the orbits of the planets? The tabernacle construction involved sensible numbers and thereafter, it just required simple arithmetic and logic to work out the size of the tent. There were also those burnt offerings whose numbers were the periods of that unique 777 day calendar. Those numbers were hidden in plain sight where they stood like zombies on parade on the landscape of scripture. It must rate as the most daring bare-faced form of encryption ever devised, yet it escaped the inquisitive prying eyes of the biblical fraternity for long over two thousand years.

In a way, the inspired biblical intelligentsia had prepared the ultimate examination test with the Celestial Tree of Knowledge and the covert data in the Old Testament for future scholars to decipher. Many scholars however believed that the treasures were real and could only have come from the temple in Jerusalem. But this stance was very misguided because several of the treasures including priestly garments, were supposed to be buried in tombs and that was sacrilegious in Jewish law as tombs were unclean and would render the treasures untouchable. Alas, nobody passed the ultimate examination test that was posed by the scribes of the copper scroll because scholars were too engrossed with the treasures. That failure shows that the biblical curriculum was utterly deficient, because it never featured an understanding of the sophisticated higher language of the scribes in the medium of time.

Astronomers across the globe have been listening on antennas for over seventy years, looking for radio signals from outer space to establish if there is intelligent life out there. It is therefore ironic that this time capsule from the caves at Qumran had miraculously survived throughout two thousand years to reveal fascinating knowledge from another world. There were many times when the structured numerical configurations with the data on astronomy on the copper scroll seemed to be in the realms of the supernatural. Such thoughts may seem out of character with the clinical grinding logic of numbers and arithmetic, but they were triggered by subliminal insights of reflection. Having left the cold theme of logic aside to look at the abilities of the visionaries in the biblical lands, it was obvious that they were spiritually guided by a higher abstract sense of awareness.

Great artists like Michelangelo with his painting of the Sistine Chapel Frescos understood this aspect of human condition, an ability to raise the human spirit to a higher level. Consider the pyramids of Egypt or the great cathedrals at York, Canterbury, Notre Dame, Chartres, The Dom in Cologne, the great buildings and art in Italy. This was the captivating work of architects and artists who understood the phenomenal mystique of the human spirit. It was an inspired feat of numerical wizardry how the biblical mathematicians programmed the 22 checksums as the first tier with Layer A utilising the numbers on the copper scroll. Sitting on top of the checksums was Layer B with the 21 periods of the calendar timetable together with the image of a cross. On top of the timetable was layer C with the orbits and long term cycles of the planets. What mortal eye looking at the data of astronomy could but believe that the writers of the copper scroll were inspired by a higher form of intelligence. To confirm this view, there was the divine autograph of YHWH on the copper scroll.

Appendix 1: Enoch's Role in Conversion of Days to Years

Those are the challenging facts that have emerged from the analysis of both the copper scroll and the Bible

Enoch played a significant role with the scribes who encoded the tables of astronomy onto the copper scroll and he was also at centre stage with Moses and the Levites. In chapter three of the Book of Numbers, Moses counted the Levites but there was a major blunder with the numbers. The Levites were broken up into three groups when they were counted in the first census with the descendants of Levi's three sons Gershom, Kohath and Merari. The number of descendants a month old or more for each son was 7,500, 8,600 and 6,200 and the total was given as 22,000. It must rate as the biggest numerical mistake in the Old Testament because the sum of those three numbers actually came to a total of 22,300. However, the subsequent analysis showed that the error was deliberate and the various numerical elements in the forthcoming equations were sanctified with strategic information that enabled a dialogue to develop, whose beauty has never been observed before by the public.

Moses had conducted the count of the Levites and he was then told by the Lord to count all the other first born Israelite males a month old or more. He did what he was told and the total came to 22,273. This figure was 273 more males than the total quoted for the Levites at 22,000. Moses was then told to redeem these 273 first born Israelites who exceeded the number of the Levites by collecting five shekels for each one. The total of 273 by 5 came to 1,365 shekels. These figures may seem to be just ordinary numbers but instead they were loaded with time period constants. To understand the body language of the biblical writers, it is necessary to look at information that is provided and deduct if there was any related element that may be noticeable only by their absence.

There are only three natural time periods, which are the solar day, lunar month and the solar year, which is 365.242 days long. (A week and a calendar month are devised periods) Two of those natural time periods were evident with the Levite census. One month was quoted as the requirement to be counted in the census and it was also practically the equivalent of the menstrual cycle. Following in its footsteps was the nine months pregnancy period of 273 days. This was where the number of the first born Israelites who exceeded the Levites was 273. That number was also the equivalent of nine solar months to the very day. Therefore, the lunar month and the solar day or days were quite evident in the biological clockworks but where was the third natural period of the 365 day year?

This third time period was not hard to detect especially where the difference between the erroneous total of 22,000 for the Lords favoured Levites and the correct total of 22,300 was 300. This figure pointed like a signpost to the Lord's most favoured person Enoch whose second age was 300 years. On the copper scroll was the number 65 and also 300 so Enoch was getting it from both scripts because his first age was given as 65 years and his second age 300 years. Just like the third natural time period, all that was missing was Enoch's final age and of course it was the number 365 albeit as years. The circuitry linking the numbers was gradually been exposed even if the ancient logic was strange to comprehend.

Another of those tell-tale omission signs was evident where the arithmetic terms of addition, subtraction and multiplication had featured in the chapter with the computations to achieve the 22,000, 273 and 1,365. But missing was the divisional factor. Therefore, the two absentees were the natural time related number of 365 and an equation to be conducted by division. Dividing a number by 365 normally implies that we are converting days to years and the clues so far suggested that this was the intended goal.

The likely candidate for this conversion was the erroneous number of 22,000. Without further ado the number 22,000 was tested to see if it really was representing days and when it was divided by 365 the result was 60.273. As decimals, the fractional element compared exactly with the 273 first born Israelites who were to be redeemed. To redeem the 273 required a donation of five shekels each and if applied to the number 60.273, the outcome would be 301.365. The result practically made up for the deficit of 300 with the real total of the Levites. Indeed, without the fractional part multiplied by 5, it would be an exact match at 300.

But the fractional part had its own profile where the high visibility solar related digits of 0.365 were now evident. However, before proceeding any further with this analysis there were some home truths about the arithmetic to be confronted. The ancients did not have decimals so they would have used fractions to produce the same result. However, the earlier equation involving 2,300 days, 1,260 days and the number 666 showed that the scribes multiplied the result by 1,000 and that gave a visibility of up to three decimal places. The same position may have been applied to this equation and the fractional part would be visible as whole numbers but taken as one thousand times smaller.

The authors left another sign where the text was at pains to stress that the shekel weighed 20 gerahs. It was if though the scribes wanted to confirm something important and in the exercise so far, what needed to be verified was that the conversion of days to years was intentional. The five shekels with its 20 gerahs multiplied out to 100. This number of 100 was the validation watermark because the 60.273 years was in fact 60 years, 100 days. Therefore, the 100 as in gerahs matched up exactly with the 100 as in days thus supporting the validity of the conversion with its outcome of 60 years 100 days.

The conversion of days to years in this article prepared the way for the analysis of the two censuses of the tribes of Israel to find a true purposes for those unbelievable population size

Bibliography

Allegro John Marco, *The Treasures of the Copper Scroll*, Routledge & Keegan, Paul, 1960

Barclay William, *The Revelation of John*, Volume 2. Published by Saint Andrew Press, Edinburgh, 1961

Davies Philip R., Brooke George J, *The Complete World of the Dead Sea Scrolls,* Callaway Phillip R. Thames & Hudson LTD, London 2002

Friedman Richard Elliot *Who Wrote the Bible*, Harper Publishers 1997

Gospel of Judas, National Geographic, Washington DC, 2008

Hack, Chad and Nathaniel Carey, *The Copper Scroll 3Q15* http://www.jewishchristianlit.com/Texts/Stud Txts/3Q15.html

Hearns, Michael; *The Messiah Immortalised in Time*, Published on www.sevenbiblewonders.com and on Amazon.

Hunger, Hermann; Pingree, David, *Astral Science in Mesopotamia,* Brill, Leiden & Boston, 1999

Josephus *The Works of Josephus*, Published by Hendrickson MA 01961-3473 USA 2001

Lefkovits Judah K, *The Copper Scroll 3Q15: A Re-evaluation*: A New Reading, Translation, and Commentary (Studies on the Texts of the Desert of Judah, Volume 25) 1999

Martínez, García, Florentino; *The Dead Sea Scrolls: Study Edition, Vol.1*. Leiden,

McLeish John *Number*, Published by Bloomsbury, London WIV 5DE 1991

Milik J. T. *Ten Years of Discovery in the Wilderness of Judaea*, SCM Press LTD, London 1959

Neugebauer, O. *The Exact Sciences in Antiquity,* New York, Dover 1969

Puech, Emile, *Le rouleau de cuivre de la grotte 3 de Qumrân (3Q15): expertise, restoration, epigraphie.* Leiden: Brill: École biblique et archéologique française de Jérusalem: EDF Foundation, 2006

Puech, Emile, *The Copper Scroll Revisited*, Brill 2015.

Sumner, Tracy Macon, *How did we get the Bible*, Barbour Publishing, USA, 2009.

VanderKam James C. *Calendars in the Dead Sea scrolls*, Publishers Rutledge, London NY 1998

Vermes Geza, *The Complete Dead Sea Scrolls in English*, Published by Penguin Books, London 2004

Whitrow GJ, *What is Time?* Publisher Thomas and Hudson, London 1972

Wise Michael, Abegg Martin, Cook Edward, *Dead Sea Scrolls*, Harper Collins, San Francisco 1999

Wolters Al *The Copper Scroll: Overview, Text and Translation*, Published by Sheffield Academic Press LTD, Sheffield S11 9AS, England 1996